# The Tabernacle
## of the Old Testament

Bobby L. Sparks, Th. D.

The Tabernacle of the Old Testament
By Bobby L. Sparks
© Copyright 2004 by Bobby L. Sparks
Greenville, TX 75402

10043

ISBN 0-9761270-0-8

Printed in the United States of America

# PREFACE

Early in my ministry, I had the opportunity to see a scale model of the tabernacle and hear lectures on the subject. I was so intrigued that I soon began my own studies. I quickly realized that the limits to the study had no boundaries and the depth of its richness had no bottom. I was ever so amazed at how much Christ was presented in the tabernacle, the priesthood and the offerings. My studies of the tabernacle have revealed Christ to be far more magnificent and glorious than I ever imagined. The more I study the subject, the greater Christ becomes to me.

There is a great personal reward in digging into the heart of the Word of God and uncovering great truths. It is my greatest desire to find these unsearchable riches of Christ and bring them to light in such simple fashion that others can see Christ in a greater way.

Bible study can be exciting. It is like digging for gold or searching for lost treasure. You may put many hard hours of effort into reading and learning, and then you find a gold nugget. Once you find one gold nugget, you go searching for another. When we study the ceremonial law and compare it to the fulfillment in Jesus Christ, we find a goldmine. There are so many beautiful illustrations depicting the life, the work, the character and the attributes of the Lord Jesus Christ. There are so many pictures of the wonder and majesty of Jesus. Why anyone who truly studies the Scriptures could find anything boring is beyond me.

Granted, there are parts to the Scriptures that are hard to understand. Because of our lack of understanding, we tend to think of some passages as boring and irrelevant. This is most common in the portions pertaining to the Jewish ceremonial law. We are inclined to feel that the ceremonial worship was a cold ritualistic worship lacking warmth and emotion. Once we embark upon an intense study, however, we discover that the opposite is true. The Levitical Law system is a gold mine of wealth when it comes to Bible study.

I am deeply indebted to my family for their part in my ministry. First, to my wife Cathy, who has been the perfect pastor's wife to help and encourage me in my ministry. Secondly, to my children, Greg, Beckie and Brian who were patient with my efforts to bring this project to completion. I cannot name all those who had a part in helping me. There were those who inspired me to dig deeper into the Word of God. There were those who helped build my original model of the tabernacle. There continue to be those who encourage me daily in my ministry. And lastly, I wish to thank the members of the Emmanuel Missionary Baptist Church of Greenville, Texas for their support to their pastor and their patience to allow him to have this ministry.

Bobby L. Sparks, ThD

# Contents

# CHAPTER ONE

# OBJECT LESSONS
# ABOUT HEAVEN

And let them make me a sanctuary; that I may dwell among them.

- Exodus 25:8

# OBJECT LESSONS
# ABOUT HEAVEN

When God began His work of creation, He had in His mind to be in the midst of His people. The Lord created a universe for man's habitation. He placed man in a most beautiful garden upon the earth. It was not long until sin marred God's plans. Sin enters the human race, and when God comes down to have His accustomed fellowship with His people, they flee from Him and hide among the trees of the garden. Man became a sinner. There was enmity, meaning hostility and unfriendliness, between God and man. Their relationship is broken and sin stands as a great barrier that separates God and mankind.

God's compassion for mankind was evident in that He wanted to dwell among them. Even though they did not necessarily seek God, He sought them.

## Man, Meet God

The purpose of the tabernacle was to provide a place and basis for which God and sinful man could mutually meet and fellowship. Man could fellowship with God as he found his way back to God and righteousness. God could fellowship with man as He shared with him His great attributes.

The tabernacle, the furniture and all that was associated with them were object lessons to the children of Israel. They were a perfect replica of something which already existed in Heaven. These were a picture, a type and a shadow of the Lord Jesus Christ, where God meets man and deity and humanity meet in one person. "Who serve unto the example and shadow of heavenly things, as Moses was admonished of God when he was about to make the tabernacle: for, See, saith he, that thou make all things according to the pattern shewed to thee in the mount" (Heb. 8:5).

## Israel's Bible In The Wilderness

The Israelites, in the early part of their history, did not have a copy of the Scriptures. They did not have the privilege of looking in the Bible and finding the chapter and verse to determine the will of the Lord. Instead, they had a series of object lessons to teach them about the Lord, about their sin, and about what they had to do to be reconciled to God. The sanctuary, the sacrifices, the priesthood, and the holy days were all intended to be object lessons to teach the Israelites all about the Lord and their responsibility to Him. These object lessons served as their Bible. The only Bible the people knew was found in the symbolisms of the ceremonial law. Everything they needed to know about the Lord, about how to be saved and serve the Lord was found in them.

## Did The Jews Understand?

We now know from the interpretation given in the book of Hebrews that all the ceremonial law pertained to Jesus Christ. The question that is often raised is did the Israelites of the Old Testament understand that all the ceremonial law was an object lesson about Jesus Christ? The answer is yes! But like so many today, the majority of Israelites were ignorant to these truths and chose to remain spiritually blind.

That the Old Testament saint could understand the significance is obvious from the Scriptures. Jesus once told a group of Jews who had access to the copies of the Old Testament parchments: "Search the scriptures; for in them ye think ye have eternal life: and they are they which testify of me" (John 5:39). Jesus went on to tell them: "For had ye believed Moses, ye would have believed me: for he wrote of me" (John 5:46). What books did Moses write? He wrote Genesis, Exodus, Leviticus, Numbers and Deuteronomy. What was he writing about? He was writing about Jesus. When Nathaniel was introducing Philip to Jesus, he said: "We have found him of whom Moses in the law, and the prophets, did write, Jesus of Nazareth" (John 1:45). The Jews who were spiritually minded understood that the ceremonial law represented Jesus Christ. Those who were not spiritually minded did not.

Only a small part of the original instructions given to Moses for the building of the tabernacle is recorded. While we have limited knowledge of the tabernacle and its significance, we must understand that the discerning Jew under the Law understood a great deal more about it than we do. Everything they needed to know about salvation and service was taught to them at the tabernacle.

It behooves me at this point to make comparison between the tabernacle and the temple. The tabernacle and the temple are exactly the same in intent and purpose. The tabernacle was a portable temple designed to be moved around in the wilderness. Once the people were well established in the land, a permanent temple was built in Jerusalem. This temple was built under the supervision of King Solomon, hence it was called Solomon's temple. The temple had the same layout and furniture as did the tabernacle. It was larger and more ornate. For purpose and significance, they were the same and to study one is to study the other.

## Mistakes Writers Make

Should one want to embark upon a study of the tabernacle, there is plenty of research material to glean from. There are many volumes on the market covering the subject. It seems that many of the writers borrow ideas and opinions from other writers. Consequently, there are some mistakes commonly made in the writings on the tabernacle. These mistakes need to be addressed. While there are varied opinions and interpretations about some of the details, there are three consistent mistakes generally taught that need to be corrected.

**Mistake Number One:**

The first and foremost mistake that most writers make is trying to make every detail in the tabernacle mean something. Writers seem to feel obligated to apply some significance to every detail. One writer made the assertion that the brass nails driven into the ground to hold up the fence and tabernacle coverings were half in the ground and half out of the ground and that it represented death and resurrection. This conclusion is only the figment of the author's imagination. It is an extreme position. When one makes such assertions without any Biblical evidence, then his credibility is brought into question on all his interpretation.

Every detail of the tabernacle probably did mean something, but we are not told what it was. Even the Apostle Paul, when writing of the sanctuary, priesthood and offerings, stated: "of which we cannot now speak particularly" (Heb. 9:5). If the Apostle Paul, both a Christian and scholar of the Law, did not understand the significance of everything, then we need to be content that neither do we. There will be questions raised in the study in which we must make a personal judgment call. We need to be honest when we express our personal opinion and when we speak for the Lord. There is so much rich material that we do know, that we do not have to assign every detail a significance and jeopardize our credibility.

## Mistake Number Two:

The second mistake is trying to make things that are similar to be necessarily symbolical of each other. There are things in the Bible that are similar. Some find similarity between some New Testament truth and the tabernacle and then conclude that the tabernacle is necessarily symbolical of that truth. This is just not always the case. One writer says the silver hooks on the fence holding up the curtains represent the church because it holds up the truth. Another says the cherubims over the mercy seat signify believers because they watch over the truth. Imaginations sometimes run wild. The New Testament church is represented by both the salt and the light, but salt does not represent light. Two separate items may very well represent a single truth, but that does not require that they represent each other.

## Mistake Number Three:

The third mistake that virtually every book on the tabernacle makes is trying to make it symbolize believers and the church. It is true that believers are found in the tabernacle, but so are unsaved sinners. The reason for this mistake is because writers take things that are similar and make them necessarily symbolical of each other.

For example, we have the seven lamp golden candlestick in the tabernacle. In the New Testament, in Revelation chapter one, we have seven golden candlesticks which are the seven churches of Asia. Virtually every book claims that the seven lamp golden candlestick in the tabernacle represents the seven churches in the book of Revelation. This is the process of making things similar necessarily symbolical of each other.

Imagine some Jewish boy asking his local priest what the candlestick represented and the priest, there in the Sinai wilderness, telling him that it represented the seven

# The Main Theme of the Tabernacle Is How Sinful Man May Approach a Holy God

| ANY INDIVIDUAL | PRIEST | HIGH PRIEST |
|---|---|---|
| COURTYARD | HOLY PLACE | HOLY OF HOLIES |

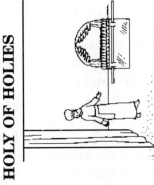

**Laver**

**Altar**

**Symbolically:**
Salvation of the soul comes when sinner brings sacrifice.
**Literally:**
When sinner accepts Christ as his sin offering in repentance.

**Symbolically:**
An ordinary priest washes at laver and enters a closer relation ship with God.
**Literally:**
Through Word of God, one is made more pure and enjoys a closer walk and relationship with the Lord.

**Symbolically:**
The high priest after sacrifice and washing enters into the very presence of God.
**Literally:**
The saint, after regeneration of both body and soul will enter into the very presence of God.

**SALVATION**      **SANCTIFICATION**      **PERFECTION**

churches of Asia. Then the boy asks: "What's a church?" and the priest answers "I don't have a clue!" The concept of a church was a total mystery to the Old Testament saint. The tabernacle had symbolism and significance intended to be understood. What purpose would it serve if it represented a mystery and impossible to understand?

In the seven lamp golden candlestick of the Old Testament, we have a beautiful picture of Jesus Christ as the light of the world. In the New Testament we have a beautiful picture of Jesus Christ as the light of the world reflected in the churches. We have two different objects, in two different ages, both a reflection of the very same thing.

If you hold your hand under a bright light against a wall, the hand will cast a shadow on the wall. The shadow bares the image of the hand. In the case of the tabernacle, the tabernacle is the shadow on the wall. Is the tabernacle the shadow of a church? No! It is a shadow of heaven. It bares the image of heaven.

The message of the tabernacle concerning Jesus Christ is the same message of the New Testament. This means that there is much similarity between the Old Testament worship and the New Testament worship. The Old Testament worship points forward to the promise of the coming Messiah. The New Testament worship is based on the promise of God that Jesus has come. One form of worship looks forward, the other looks backward. Let us not make the mistake of making the tabernacle be a type and shadow of the church. Many writers claim that washing at the laver before entering the tabernacle is a picture of baptism before entering the church. It is true, there is some similarity, but if you take this too far, you will have pouring and sprinkling water a symbol of New Testament baptism.

## The Interpretation by Scripture

We do well if we merely allow the Scriptures to interpret the spiritual meanings of the tabernacle. We are not
left to our imagination and opinion as to the significance.

Hebrews chapters eight, nine and ten give us the
interpretation. Hebrews 8:5 uses three words to describe
the significance of the sanctuary: "Who serve unto the
example and shadow of heavenly things, as Moses was
admonished of God when he was about to make the tabernacle: for , See, saith he, that thou make all things according to the pattern shewed to thee in the mount." Hebrews
9:9 uses a different term: "Which was a figure for the time
then present, in which were offered both gifts and sacrifices, that could not make him that did the service perfect,
as pertaining to the conscience."

The significance of the tabernacle is repeated in
Hebrews 9:23-24: "It was therefore necessary that the
patterns of things in the heavens should be purified with
these; but the heavenly things themselves with better sacrifices than these. For Christ is not entered into the holy
place made with hands, which are the figures of the true;
but into heaven itself, now to appear in the presence of
God for us:" Lastly, Hebrews 10:1 states that the "law
having a shadow of good things to come, and not the very
image of the things."

The words "example," "shadow," "figure," and "pattern"
are used. The word "example" is from a word in which we
get "copy." A copy is merely a duplicate of the original. A
figure is a visible form of another object. A shadow is a
dark image cast by the obstruction of light. A pattern is
not the original object, but is made from the original. All
these terms indicate that the tabernacle or temple is not
the original, but an image of the original. The original is
heaven, and the tabernacle is a copy or shadow of it.

One of the frustrating things about studying all the
books and material on the tabernacle is that the writers

pick one item and say that it means "this" and pick another item and say it means "that." But "this" and "that" have absolutely no relation to each other. Many fail to realize there is one central theme to the tabernacle and everything in it has to harmonize with that one theme. The layout, the construction, the furniture and all the ceremonies of the tabernacle all blend together as the notes in the melody of a song. They are in perfect sequence and symmetry. Such perfect harmony could only be designed in the mind of God. When once we understand the one main theme, then we can best understand the significance of items not specifically stated. Our personal opinions will be more accurate with a genuine understanding of the main theme.

The tabernacle is a building with two rooms: the Holy Place and the Holy of Holies. The Holy of Holies represents God's throne in heaven and His presence there. Around the building is a courtyard enclosed by a fence. On the outside of the fence is a nation, literally a world, of sinful people. The main theme of the tabernacle is how that wicked, sinful man may enter into the presence of a holy and just God and fellowship with Him.

## Six Aspects of the Central Theme

### The Sinful Depravity of Man

With that being the case, there are several aspects of this main theme. There are six things we may glean from the central subject. First of all, man is taught his sinful depravity by being shut out from the presence of God and having to offer various sacrifices to redeem himself. One of the major lessons from a study of the tabernacle is just how sinful man is. Because of his sins, he is shut out from the presence of God. He has sinned and the penalty for his sins is eternal separation from God. This study reduces man to the vile, wicked sinner that he is. There is nothing good to say about him (Rom. 3:23; Psalm 51:5; Isa. 64:6; Rom. 3:12).

## God is Good

Secondly, we learn of the greatness of the Lord's holiness and righteousness. God is a holy and just God and there is a great gulf between Himself and mankind.

False religion is based upon error on the above two points. False religion lowers God to a level in which He does not belong. It raises man to a level to which he is not entitled, so that there is little difference between God and man. Those who teach works for salvation do not understand either God's great righteousness and holiness, nor man's sinful depravity.

## Man Must Change

Thirdly, the tabernacle pictures the great change man must experience in order for man to enter into the presence and fellowship with the Lord. God will not stoop to our level. Man has to be raised to God's level. This change is so great that God has to make the change in mankind. From what he presently is, man must encounter a great change so as to be able to be reconciled with God.

## The Terms of Man's Approach to God

Fourth, we learn in the tabernacle the terms how sinful man could be reconciled and approach a holy and just God. It is man that has sinned against God. The Lord has the right to set the terms of our reconciliation. Through entering the gate, the sacrifice at the altar, the washing at the laver, and the bringing in blood into the sanctuary all represent the terms of man's reconciliation and his right to come before the Lord.

## The Plan of Salvation

Fifth, we learn the plan of salvation necessary for man to be redeemed from his sins. The slaying of the innocent animal sacrifices taught that a penalty had to be paid for being a sinner and committing sins, and that the penalty was death. The plan of salvation in the Old Testament is exactly the same plan of salvation in the New Testament. If we polled Christians and asked how people were saved in the Old Testament many would respond that one was saved by offering sacrifices at the altar and keeping the law. That answer is a thousand times wrong! There has been only one plan of salvation for all ages. If man could have been saved by keeping the law, then our churches would have an altar in the front yard and a pen of goats in the back yard and we would still be offering sacrifices. The necessity of having to offer sacrifices indicated that the offerer was a sinner and needed a substitute to die in his place. The sacrifices only represented Jesus Christ, who would be the Lamb of God that takes away the sin of the world. "Neither by the blood of goats and calves, but by his own blood he entered in once into the holy place, having obtained eternal redemption for us" (Heb. 9:12).

Through the ceremonial law of the Old Testament, the people were promised that Jesus Christ would come and die for their sins. In the New Testament, people are promised that Jesus Christ has come and died for our sins. They believed He would. We believe He has. It is the same faith for both. God promised, and God cannot lie, that every sinner who repented and believed in Jesus would be saved. He was able to save those in the Old Testament even before Christ died on the cross.

## Christ is the Theme

Sixth, the tabernacle was a figure and type of the Lord Jesus Christ. It represents His work, His life, His attributes and His character. Every detail of the tabernacle pre-figured and foreshadowed some aspect of the infinite character and work of the Lord Jesus Christ. Jesus Christ and His redemptive work is the theme of the tabernacle.

The tabernacle in the wilderness was a figure and shadow of Jesus Christ. The brazen altar speaks of Him on the cross. The laver speaks of Him as the Word. The table of showbread speaks of Him as the bread of life and the candlestick as the Light of the world. The altar of incense speaks of Him as our interceding High Priest. The ark speaks of His attribute of justice, and the mercy seat tells of His attribute of love and mercy. The wood speaks of His perfect humanity, and the gold tells of His deity. Brass tells of His judgment, and silver reveals His redemption. White speaks of His perfect righteousness; scarlet tells of His shed blood; and purple suggests His royalty. The vail speaks of His perfect life and standard of righteousness, and the list goes on.

The tabernacle on earth is a type of the tabernacle in Heaven. The dwelling place of God on earth is a shadow of the dwelling place of God in Heaven.

# CHAPTER TWO

**West**

Ephraim
Manasseh
Benjamin

*Gershonites*

**South**

*Kohathites*

Reuben
Simeon
Gad

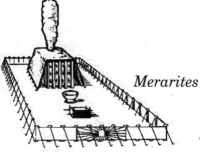

*Merarites*

*Priests*

**North**

Dan
Asher
Naphtali

Judah
Issachar
Zebulun

**East**

# SQUARELY IN THE
# MIDDLE

Every man of the children of Israel shall pitch by his own standard, with the ensign of their father's house: far off about the tabernacle of the congregation shall they pitch.

**Numbers 2:2**

But the Levites after the tribe of their fathers were not numbered among them.

For the LORD had spoken unto Moses, saying,

Only thou shalt not number the tribe of Levi, neither take the sum of them among the children of Israel:

But thou shalt appoint the Levites over the tabernacle of testimony, and over all the vessels thereof, and over all things that [belong] to it: they shall bear the tabernacle, and all the vessels thereof; and they shall minister unto it, and shall encamp round about the tabernacle.

**Numbers 1:47-50**

# SQUARELY IN THE MIDDLE

Where God chose to place the tabernacle in relation to the tribes of Israel when they camped is highly significant, both physically and spiritually. The camp, as all other aspects of the tabernacle, was arranged in the order ordained by God.

## The Tabernacle Faced East

Each time they would set up camp, the tabernacle was always positioned so that the entrance was always facing the eastward direction (Ex. 38:13-14; Num. 2:3; 3:38). They were never permitted to face the tabernacle any other direction for any reason.

In the instruction recorded by Moses no reason is stated for this easterly requirement. The direction of east was significant to the Jews. The priests camped on the east side. The royal tribe of Judah camped on the east side. When the portable tabernacle was replaced by the permanent temple built by Solomon, it also faced the easterly direction. When Solomon's temple was replaced by Zerubbabel's temple which was later remodeled by Herod and called Herod's temple, it too faced the direction of east.

Ezekiel the prophet, while in exile in Babylon, was given visions of the happenings going on within Israel. He saw the corruption of the Israelites. The situation was so bad that God ordered the destruction of Israel and the city of Jerusalem. In a vision, Ezekiel saw the glory of the Lord depart the temple in Jerusalem. He reported that the Lord departed by the way of the east (Ezek. 10:18-19; 11:23).

Ezekiel further prophesied of the Lord's return to the earth to dwell in the midst of Israel during the millennium. He reported: "And the glory of the Lord came into the house (temple) by the way of the east" (Ezek. 43:4).

We are also taught that our outlook should be eastward, towards the rising of the sun, from whence the Lord will make His appearing. Jesus said: "For as the lightning cometh out of the east ... so shall also the coming of the Son of man be" (Matt. 24:27). Ezekiel's prophecy and Christ's claim to come again is one and the same. Jesus further said: "When the Son of man shall come in his glory, and all the holy angels with him, then shall he sit upon the throne of his glory" (Matt. 25:31).

The position of the tabernacle facing east was a prophetic declaration that pointed to the coming of Jesus Christ to dwell among His people. This is why He said: "Let them make me a sanctuary that I may dwell among them" (Ex. 25:8). The Israelites in the wilderness were constantly reminded to look forward to the coming of the Messiah. This is why the Lord said: "Let them make me a sanctuary; that I may dwell among them" (Ex. 25:8).

## The Position of the Twelve Tribes
## Around the Tabernacle

> And the LORD spake unto Moses and unto Aaron, saying, Every man of the children of Israel shall pitch by his own standard, with the ensign of their father's house: far off about the tabernacle of the congregation shall they pitch.
>
> Numbers 2:1-2

The tabernacle was always to be central, with an encampment of some two-and-one-half million people covering a circuit of about twelve miles. The tents were pitched in a carefully prescribed formation very much like a military camp. Everything centered around the tabernacle. Without the tabernacle, there would have been no plan or order to the camp. There would have been nothing but a constantly changing, shifting, unsettled conglomeration and disorderly mob.

According to Numbers 2:2, there was a reserved space between the twelve tribes and the tabernacle. This space was allocated for two reasons. First, the tribe of Levi, divided into four groups, was to make their camps on all four sides between the tabernacle and the other tribes. Even in the camp arrangement, the Levites as the priestly tribe was the "go-between" between the people and the Lord. Secondly, part of this vacant space was where the elders of the people would assemble for national meetings before God for worship and instruction.

### The East Side Camp

On the east side of the tabernacle camped the tribes of Judah, Issachar and Zebulun (Num. 2:3-9). Judah was the standard-bearer of this camp. When the hosts of Israel set forth on the march, this camp led the way.

### The South Side Camp

On the south side camped the tribes of Reuben, Simeon and Gad (Num. 2:10-16). Reuben was the standard-bearer for this camp. When the people set forth on the move, these went in second place.

### The West Side Camp

On the west side camped the tribes of Ephraim, Manasseh and Benjamin (Num. 2:18-24). Ephraim was the standard-bearer for this camp. They were the fourth group to go on the march because the tribe of Levi, bearing the tabernacle went third in the march.

## The North Side Camp

On the north side camped the tribes of Dan, Asher and Naphtali (Num. 2:25-31). Dan was the standard-bearer for this group. On the march, this group was the fifth and brought up the rear.

On each side surrounding the tabernacle, one tribe displayed its standard that the other tribes might follow and know their camp position. The standard-bearing tribes were: Judah, Reuben, Ephraim and Dan. All the tribes of Israel had their family emblems but only these tribes were significant in the arrangement of the camp around the tabernacle.

The Hebrew word translated "standard" is also translated "banner." This standard was probably a figure or device of some kind elevated on a pole or perhaps a flag. There is no indication as to what emblem was on these standards in the Scriptures specifically pertaining to the tabernacle; however, there are some implications that are highly suggestive of some possible emblems.

Since the tabernacle symbolically represents the throne of God in the Heavens, a scene in Heaven might indicate the significance of these standards. Such a scene is found in Ezekiel chapter one. In verse 10 it is written: "As for the likeness of their faces, they four had the face of a man, and the face of a lion, on the right side: and they four had the face of an ox on the left side; they four also had the face of an eagle." Ezekiel was describing the throne of God and the "four living creatures" that continually surrounded the throne.

When John saw the throne of God in Heaven, he reported the following: "And the first beast was like a lion, and the second beast like a calf, and the third beast had a face as a man, and the fourth beast was like a flying eagle" (Rev. 4:7). John was describing a scene around the throne of God in Heaven. The creatures of John's vision are the same as Ezekiel's.

These prophetic scenes in Heaven and the living creatures surrounding God's throne are highly suggestive that the standards around the throne of God on earth bore the same emblems. Evidence from the Scriptures further indicate the emblems on the standards were the same as the four creatures.

The standard for the tribe of Judah was the lion. In his blessing of Judah, Jacob made this statement regarding him: "Judah is a lion's whelp: from the prey, my son, thou are gone up: he stooped down, he couched as a lion, and as an old lion; who shall rouse him up?" (Gen. 49:9).

The symbol depicted upon the standard of Reuben was a human head because Reuben was the firstborn and the head of the family. Furthermore, Jacob said that Reuben was "unstable as water," which is characteristic of man (Gen. 49:4). Above the camp of Ephraim, on the standard, the head of a calf was depicted because it was through the vision of the calves that his ancestor Joseph had predicted and provided for the famine in Egypt (Gen. 41). In blessing the tribe of Joseph, that is, Ephraim, Moses said: "His glory is like the firstling of his bullock" (Deut. 33:17).

The family crest for Dan was quite possibly an eagle, the great foe to serpents, which had been chosen in the place of a serpent because his forefather Jacob had compared Dan to a serpent saying, "Dan shall be a serpent by the way, and adder in the path" (Gen. 49:17). The family could have substituted the eagle, the destroyer of serpents, rather than carrying an adder upon their standard. This within itself is deceiving, which is the very character of Dan.

These four emblems on the standards represent supremacy in some form. Man represents supremacy over all created life. The lion represents supremacy over all untamed life as the "king of beasts." The ox represents supremacy over all domestic life, and the eagle is the king over the fowls of the air. As these emblems appear in the scenes of Heaven around the throne of God, they represent

God's supremacy over all creatures and creation in every direction. "Great is our Lord, and of great power: his understanding is infinite" (Psalm 147:5).

## The Position of the Levite
## Surrounding the Tabernacle

The tribe of Levi was not numbered among the tribes of Israel to receive an inheritance. Pertaining to this, the Scriptures state:

> But the Levites after the tribe of their fathers were not numbered among them.
> For the LORD had spoken unto Moses, saying,
> Only thou shalt not number the tribe of Levi, neither take the sum of them among the children of Israel:
> But thou shalt appoint the Levites over the tabernacle of testimony, and over all the vessels thereof, and over all things that [belong] to it: they shall bear the tabernacle, and all the vessels thereof; and they shall minister unto it, and shall encamp round about the tabernacle.
>                                                    Numbers 1:47-50

Since Levi was one of the sons of Jacob and was not numbered among the children of Israel, only eleven sons were left to receive an inheritance. Yet, twelve tribes surround the tabernacle. An examination of the twelve tribes will reveal that the two sons of Joseph, Ephraim and Manasseh, receive an inheritance equal to the others (Gen. 49:1-22). The names of Ephraim and Manasseh appear in the list of tribes to replace the names Joseph and Levi.

The  family of Levi was divided into four groups consisting of the priests and three family heads. These groups were stationed between the other tribes of Israel and the tabernacle. "But the Levites shall pitch round about the tabernacle of testimony, that there be no wrath upon the congregation of the children of Israel: and the

Levites shall keep the charge of the tabernacle of testimony (Num. 1:53). Levi had three sons: Kohath, Gershon and Merari. Moses and Aaron were of the family of Kohath. The family of priests descended from the family of Aaron.

## The Camp of the Priests

Aaron, as the high priest, and the other priests were camped on the east side, next to the entrance. "But those that encamp before the tabernacle toward the east, even before the tabernacle of the congregation eastward, shall be Moses and Aaron and his sons, keeping the charge of the sanctuary for the charge of the children of Israel; and the stranger that cometh nigh shall be put to death" (Num. 3:38). The priests had the overall supervision of the tabernacle. They conducted the various ceremonies as well as supervised the maintenance and putting up and taking down of the tabernacle.

The three sons of Levi were positioned with their families around the perimeter of the tabernacle. The Levite families of Kohath, Gershon and Merari were located in the area between the tabernacle and the other twelve tribes. Each family had designated duties appertaining to the maintenance and moving of the tabernacle.

## The Camp of the Kohathites

The Kohathites were camped on the south side. They were charged with the care of the furniture, that is, the ark and mercy seat, the vail, the brazen altar, the brazen laver, the candlestick, the table of shewbread and the altar of incense (Num. 3:29-31). Though the Gershonites were in charge of all other hangings, the Kohathites were charged with the vail, as it also served as a covering over the ark and mercy seat during a move. Due to the fact that the furniture had provisions to be carried by staves upon the shoulders of the men, no equipment was given to them to transport the items (Num. 7:9).

## The Camp of the Gershonites

The Gershonites were camped on the west side. They were responsible for the putting up and taking down of the coverings over the tabernacle, the hangings, the fence and all the cords (Num. 3:23, 25-26). They were provided with two wagons and four oxen to equip them in the transporting of the tabernacle (Num. 7:7).

## The Camp of the Merarites

The Merarites were camped on the north side. They had charge and custody of the boards, bars, pillars, sockets, bases and all that pertained to them (Num. 3:35-37). The Merarites were equipped with four wagons and eight oxen to transport that which was under their charge (Num. 7:8).

The Israelites would be well settled in their camp, when suddenly the cloud above the tabernacle would begin to rise and move. The priests would enter the tabernacle area to supervise the disassembling of it. They would cover the furniture and prepare it for the move. The Kohathites would enter first and remove the furniture upon their shoulders. The Gershonites would follow removing the linen fence, the coverings, the hangings and so forth and load it on their wagons. Immediately behind them, the Merarites would take down the posts to the fence, remove the bars from the tabernacle boards and then load them on their wagons. With each group and man having a specific job, it was quite possible that the tabernacle would be disassembled within three hours and reassembled within a day. There were over nine-thousand-six-hundred eligible Levites qualified to this work.

The fact that the tabernacle was placed squarely in the center of the camp reveals that God came to dwell not only among the people, but in the very midst of them. God was the very theme for the very existence of the nation. He was their leader, their God. Their existence, their laws, their rituals and practices, their ordinances, even their lives were all centered around the Lord. Since the tabernacle was a type of Christ, we conclude that the Messiah, the Savior of mankind, was the basis of their existence.

## The Vacant Space

There was a certain distance maintained between the camps of Israel and the tabernacle. "Far off about the tabernacle of the congregation shall they pitch" (Num. 2:2). The Levites were stationed between the other twelve tribes and the tabernacle and the reason is stated: "That there be no wrath upon the congregation of the children of Israel" (Num. 1:53).

The nation of Israel was a sinful nation, as Paul says they "were by nature the children of wrath" (Eph. 2:3). Because of this, they had to camp "afar off." They could not come nigh unto the tabernacle without an offering to make atonement for their sins. It is through the offering of Jesus Christ that mankind could come close and approach God. Paul went on to say: "But now in Christ Jesus ye who sometimes were far off are made nigh by the blood of Christ" (Eph. 2:13). This distance between the camps and the tabernacle was designed to expose the sinfulness of the people and, because of that, they were isolated from the Lord.

# CHAPTER THREE

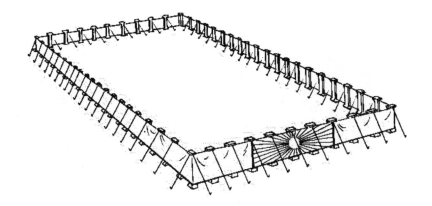

# THE PRECINCTS OF
# THE TABERNACLE

And the LORD went before them by day in a pillar of a cloud, to lead them the way; and by night in a pillar of fire, to give them light; to go by day and night:

He took not away the pillar of the cloud by day, nor the pillar of fire by night, [from] before the people.

**Exodus 13:21-22**

# THE PRECINCTS OF THE TABERNACLE

The Israelites were to be recompensed for the many years of slavery they spent in Egyptian bondage. Upon leaving Egypt, they were paid what was fairly due them by "spoiling" the Egyptians (Ex. 12:35-36). They were paid in one day for hundreds of years of slavery.

The Lord called on Israel to make freewill donations from these spoils that the tabernacle might be built (Ex. 35:21-29). They brought so willingly, so gladly, so bountifully that the men charged with the responsibility of receiving the gifts had to go to Moses and tell him: "The people bring much more than enough for the service of the work, which the Lord commanded to make" (Ex. 36:5; Cf. Ex. 36:6-7).

God called upon the people to bring their offerings for the tabernacle with a willing heart and as their spirits stirred them up, and they brought more than was needed for the work. The condition of our heart is reflected in our willingness to give to the cause of the Lord.

## The Skilled Workers

Moses was naturally in charge of the overall construction of the tabernacle, the furniture, the vessels and even the garments of the priests. But the actual construction was left to special skilled workers and the people. God's requirements in building and design were more than naturally talented men could produce. The skill and artistic work put into the tabernacle is beyond that of natural ability of any person living in any age.

It was necessary for God to call and equip men with special gifted abilities to build the tabernacle in the manner in which God required. The men, their call and their gifts are listed in Exodus 35:30-35.

The name of Bezaleel means "in the shadow of God." The other principal workman was Aholiab whose name means "tent of my father." Not only did they have the skills to perform work not able to be accomplished by natural man, but they were able to teach these skills to others.

## The Cloud by Day and Pillar of Fire by Night

Upon leaving Egypt, the Lord provided Israel with a canopy of a cloud by day and a pillar of fire by night. As they traveled by day, the cloud provided a cool shadowing cover. It most likely provided protection from the ultraviolet rays of the sun. With the low humidity of the desert and an umbrella of a cloud the travel was not so uncomfortable. Then, at night, the cloud lighted up the camp and the people were able to accomplish many of their domestic duties with the presence of the light.

When Pharaoh realized that the children of Israel had left Egypt, he determined to pursue after them. He pursued them as far as the Red Sea and there found them encamped. At once, the pillar of cloud changed its position. Instead of going before them, it went behind them and stood between them and the Egyptians (Ex. 14:19-20). The Egyptians were unable to come after the Israelites and they crossed the Red Sea over dry ground. During the night, the cloud was removed and the Egyptian army pursued after them in the sea. The sea returned upon them, engulfed them and the entire army perished in the water.

From there, the pillar of cloud led them to Sinai where the Israelites entered into a covenant relationship with the Lord as a nation. The cloud abode with them during the forty days Moses was in the mountain receiving instructions for the Law and the building of the sanctuary. It abode with them during the next seven months of construction of the tabernacle. When the tabernacle was finished and all things in order, the cloud covered it as it is written:

> Then a cloud covered the tent of the congregation, and the glory of the LORD filled the tabernacle.
> And Moses was not able to enter into the tent of the congregation, because the cloud abode thereon, and the glory of the LORD filled the tabernacle.
> And when the cloud was taken up from over the tabernacle, the children of Israel went onward in all their journeys:
> But if the cloud were not taken up, then they journeyed not till the day that it was taken up.
> For the cloud of the LORD [was] upon the tabernacle by day, and fire was on it by night, in the sight of all the house of Israel, throughout all their journeys.
> Exodus 40:34-38; Cf. Numbers 9:15-22.

Once the tabernacle was built, furnished and equipped for worship, the cloud descended upon it (Ex. 40:34-38). The presence of the cloud indicated when it was time to pack up the sanctuary and travel to the next location. We do not know exactly how it happened, but somehow the cloud, in some special manner, hovered over the sanctuary. When the cloud lifted up, it was time to pack up and move. As the cloud began to move, the Israelites would follow it. There was no indication as to where it would go and when it would stop. The people entirely depended on the cloud to direct them in their journeyings through the wilderness. (Cf. Num. 10:11-12).

Questions are sometimes raised pertaining to the priests entering the tabernacle and going into the Holy of Holies especially when it is specified that only the High

Priest could enter there once a year on the Day of
Atonement. Sometimes writers speak of the shekinah
light that that appeared over the mercy seat and between
the cherubim. We must understand that the shekinah
light was literally the cloud that descended into the Holy
of Holies and appeared as a light between the cherubim
(Lev. 16:2). The presence of the Lord was made know
when the cloud descended upon the tabernacle. When the
cloud went up, then the priests could enter the Holy of
Holies and cover and remove the ark of the covenant and
mercy seat. Without the presence of the cloud, the priests
were free to enter all parts of the sanctuary.

The presence of almighty God is seen in the tabernacle. God is a triune God of three personalities: God the
Father, God the Son and God the Holy Spirit. The cloud
might symbolically represent the Holy Spirit and His
work might be deducted from the basis and use of the pillar of cloud and fire that overshadowed Israel. The cloud
was the light in the darkness, as the Holy Spirit is light
in the darkness (1 John 1:5). The cloud was the guide
through the wilderness, as the Holy Spirit is our Guide
(John 16:13). The cloud was evidence of the Lord's presence, as the Holy Spirit gives evidence of the Lord's presence (John 16:13-14). The cloud never left the people, as
the Lord promised through the Spirit never to leave us
(Heb. 13:5). The cloud brought comfort to the Israelites by
His presence, as the Holy Spirit is also our Comforter
(John 14:16-18).

God guided His people by simply moving the cloud
when He wanted Israel to move and stopping the cloud in
the spot He wanted them to stay. Today, God wants to lead
His people just as definitely and deliberately by His presence, the Holy Spirit. "For as many as are led by the Spirit
of God, they are the sons of God" (Rom. 8: 14). "If ye be led
of the Spirit" (Gal. 5:18). Oh, the joys of walking in con-
scious dependence upon the Holy Spirit and seeing Him
direct your steps to the spot He wants you. There is grave

danger in not moving when God leads, but this is also true about moving when God does not lead. It would save many heartaches and much loss if Christians would consciously wait on the Lord before making decisions and running out of His will.

## Three Areas Of The Tabernacle

### The Courtyard

There were three main areas to the precincts of the tabernacle. The outer area just inside the fence was known as the courtyard. Any person could enter the courtyard provided he or she brought an animal sacrifice. One could not go down to the tabernacle and enter the courtyard just to look around and observe the rituals. No one was allowed to enter the courtyard without a sacrifice.

### The Holy Place

The second area is called the Holy Place. The tabernacle building consisted of two rooms. In order to enter the second room, the priest had to go through the first room. The first room in the tabernacle was the Holy Place. Only the priests could enter the Holy Place, and only then could they enter it after they washed their hands and their feet at the laver in the courtyard. The priests entered this room several times each day.

### The Holy of Holies

The third main area is called the Holy of Holies. It is the second room of the tabernacle building. Only the high priest could enter here on the annual Day of Atonement.

# The Courtyard Fence

The tabernacle and a certain amount of area surrounding it were enclosed by means of a courtyard fence.
The only entrance into the courtyard and into the tabernacle was by a gate provided at the eastern end.

The fence had a length of one-hundred cubits on the
north and south sides and fifty cubits on the east and west
sides. Using eighteen inches as a standard of measure-
ment for a cubit, the courtyard fence enclosed an area
one-hundred-fifty feet long by seventy-five feet wide. The
height of the fence was five cubits or seven and one-half
feet. Without counting the special hanging for the
entrance, the total length of the linen curtain was two
hundred eighty cubits, which was exactly the same length
of the linen covering over the top of the tabernacle.

## The Pillars

The north and south sides of the fence each contained
twenty pillars, and the west and east side each had ten
pillars, making a total of sixty pillars. Very little is ever
said about the positioning of these pillars. Among those
who do comment on them, there is much discrepancy. In
taking into consideration the total number of pillars and
the total distance, the only reasonable conclusion is that
the pillars are positioned exactly five cubits apart, the
same as the height of the fence.

The problem that most have with the pillars is counting the corner posts. Along the length is twenty pillars,
and along the width is ten pillars. One each corner is a
post that can be seen from two sides. The corner posts are
not counted twice, and only one is counted with each side.
An exact distance of five cubits between each pillar will
give exactly the total distance and number of posts
required.

## The Fence Material

The fence was made of a variety of materials. The basic fence itself consisted of a curtain of "fine twined linen." The fence, or curtain as it was called, was hung upon sixty "pillars" or posts. Each pillar was set in a brass socket or base. Attached to the top of each pillar were silver "chapiters," or caps on top of the posts. For the purpose of connecting the curtain to the pillars, silver "hooks" and "fillets" were used. Exactly how the hooks were attached to the curtain and pillars is not known.

The exact identity of the "fillets" is not clear. The original Hebrew word means "joinings, to bind, connect, clasp." They were most likely rods or poles which connected the pillars from which the curtains were suspended. These rods would provide greater stability to the fence and prevent the curtain from sagging between the posts.

The fence was stabilized by means of tent pegs or "pins" made of brass and "cords." Each pillar was secured by two cords, one on the inside of the fence and one on the outside. These cords were attached to the top of the pillar and extended down to one of the pins.

The pillars were very likely made of acacia (shittim) wood. There were no recorded instructions designating the material of which the posts were to be made. Some think they may have been made of brass, but the total amount of brass used in the tabernacle does not allow for that much to be used in the posts. Since the rest of the columns and boards were without exception made of wood, it is the most likely material for the posts as well.

The wood commonly used throughout the tabernacle was shittim wood (pronounced "sheet-tem"), most commonly known as "acacia" wood. The acacia tree is sometimes found to be three or four feet in diameter and grows to be as much as twenty feet high. The wood is close-grained and very hard. It is naturally a blonde color and turns a reddish-brown after it is cut. It continues to dark-en with age. It grows remarkably well in dry places, and is highly insect resistant. Because of its durability the Septagtuint translated it "incorruptible wood."

Each of the posts were standing in a base of brass. The Hebrew word *nechoseth* is the basic word translated "copper, bronze and brass." Copper is a pure element, bronze is a mixture of copper and tin, and brass is a mixture of copper and zinc. Copper naturally was first put to use. The bronze age appeared before Abraham. And brass, which is comparatively modern, did appear in rare usages as early as 1500 B.C. The original word does not lend proof as to whether the metal used in the tabernacle was actually copper, bronze or brass. The basic element in bronze or brass is copper, and any significance is probably found in the copper.

The weight of the brass that was dedicated to the Lord as a wave-offering totaled seventy talents and 2,400 shekels, which is about three and one-half tons (Ex. 38:29). At today's value the copper would be worth about $5,500.00. This metal is known for its exceptional strength and its high resistance to fire. Its melting point is 1,985 degrees Fahrenheit. Curiously, the word "brass" and the word "serpent" are the same word in Hebrew. Whether they are derived from the same root word or meaning is not clear.

## The Gate

In order for man to enter the tabernacle, or the courtyard, he had to come through the gate. The gate was located on the east side. The width of the gate was twenty cubits (thirty feet), and the height was five cubits (seven and one-half feet). Four pillars were designated to hold the gate curtain. Theses pillars, bases, the caps, the pins, the cords and the fillets were the same as the rest of the fence. The only difference between the gate and the rest of the fence was the hanging or curtain. This curtain was made of blue, purple, scarlet and fine twined (white) linen.

This gate hanging has much in common with the other hangings of the tabernacle. It will be specifically dealt with in both description and significance under a separate title called "the hangings of the tabernacle."

## The Significance

In spiritual significance, the linen fence, white and clean represents the sinlessness and righteousness of Jesus Christ. Linen is a fabric woven from thread made of the fine fibers of the flax plant. The Egyptians were especially famous for their weaving fine linen. This particular linen was the highest quality and very expensive. Flax was also introduced into Jericho (Joshua 2:6) and also in Galilee. The flax stalk grew quite tall and was about the size of a drinking straw. It was cut or pulled out by the roots near full growth, dried for a time in the sun, then pounded vigorously to separate the fine fibers, washed and then bleached. The fiber, so fine at times as to be almost invisible, was then ready for the weaver. The weavers in Palestine were able to make linen almost as fine as silk.

In the New Testament, the word for linen is *bussos*. There are several words translated linen in the Old Testament from the Hebrew. With regard to the tabernacle, the word linen is from the Hebrew *shesh*. None of the other words for linen apply to the tabernacle itself, but at least two apply to the dress of the priests. *Shesh* means "fine linen" and comes from a root word meaning "whiteness" because of its brilliant white color. This linen is the highest quality of linen that man has ever produced. They would pick through all the flax fibers and choose only the perfectly white fibers for this fabric. It was labor intense to produce this quality linen. It is cost prohibitive to produce today. Even in Bible days, it was only worn by the royal and wealthy.

There is another Hebrew word translated linen used in connection with, but not in the actual construction of the tabernacle. That word is *bad*, and comes from a root word meaning "separation." This linen was used in a part of the garments of the priests. It is the common linen worn by the common person. For the most part, all the garments of the priests were of the *shesh* linen. But the breeches of the priests (or the under pants) was of *bad* linen. When the pries would take out the ashes from the altar, he would change from a garment made of *shesh* linen and change into a garment made of *bad* linen. And, then, on the annual Day of Atonement, the high priest would change from his elaborate dress made of *shesh* linen to a very simple garment made of *bad* linen to carry on his duties for that day.

The above two words for linen are very consistently used so as not to be confused with each other. There is a third Hebrew word translated linen. It is *pishtah* and is a generic word for flax or linen. It is not used in connection with the tabernacle or priests in any way. However, it is used in connection with the linen garments of the priests in the millennial temple (Ezek. 44:17-18). It could apply to any quality or type of linen.

There can be no question of the significance of fine linen. It tells of the spotlessness, holiness, purity, righteousness of the Lord Jesus, manifested in every act, word and thought of His daily life (Heb. 7:26).

The fact that fine linen represents righteousness is clearly stated in the Scriptures. It says in Revelation 19:7-8: "The marriage of the Lamb is come, and his wife hath made herself ready. And to her was granted that she should be arrayed in fine linen, clean and white: for the fine linen is the righteousness of saints."

Here is the verdict from the Scriptures. Pilate said: "I find no fault in this man" (Luke 23:4). Pilate's wife said: "Have thou nothing to do with that just man" (Matt. 27:19). Judas Iscariot said: "I have sinned in that I have betrayed innocent blood" (Matt. 27:4). The thief on the cross said: "This man hath done nothing amiss" (Luke 23:41). The centurion at the cross said: "Certainly this was a righteous man" (Luke 23:47). Peter said: "Who knew no sin, neither was guile found in his mouth" (1 Peter 2:22). The heavenly Father said: "My beloved Son, in whom I am well pleased" (Matt. 17:5). Paul, the apostle said: "Holy, harmless, undefiled, separate from sinners" (Heb. 7:26). And Jesus challenged His critics: "Which of you convinceth me of sin?" (John 8:46).

The silver caps, hooks and rods portray Christ as the payment or atonement price for our sins. The brass pins and bases depict Christ bearing the judgment of our sins and perhaps being the judge of our sins. Throughout the tabernacle, the wood illustrates Christ in His humanity, and the gold illustrates His deity.

In looking upon the fence as a whole, the enclosure made a clean separation between the inside and outside, between God and man. As in any fence, it served the purpose to separate and to set boundaries. Without doubt, there is depicted design intended in the fence. As the linen represents righteousness, we are made to realize that the righteousness of God is a barrier that prevents natural man from being in His presence. God's presence cannot be contaminated by sin; so He was shut in from the world and the world was shut out from Him.

Just imagine! Someone goes through the camp of Israel and informs the people that the tabernacle is finished and that Almighty God now dwells in the midst of the camp of Israel. One of the Israelites, excited at the prospect of seeing and meeting God, bursts out in a run to go to the tabernacle. Picture him as he excitedly runs through the camp and darts between the dwellings and breaks out into the opening where the tabernacle sits. Picture him as he jerks to a sudden stop immediately in front of the fence. There in front of him is a great white fence. The presence of that fence declares: "Danger! Do Not Enter!" The British have a unique way of saying it: "Enter under pain of death." No sign could make it any more clear "Keep Out!"

But, was not the fence against the whole nature of the tabernacle? Was not the tabernacle erected to provide God a dwelling place among men? Did not God desire to reestablish fellowship between Himself and fallen man? And was not the tabernacle, the priesthood and the offerings provided that a place and basis could be made for which God and man could mutually meet and fellowship?

The nature and character of man is clearly established in Isaiah 64:6: "But we are all as an unclean thing, and all our righteousnesses are as filthy rags; and we all do fade as a leaf; and our iniquities, like the wind, have taken us away." Righteousness and unrighteousness have no fellowship together (2 Cor. 6:14). Habakkuk describes God's character and nature when he said: "Thou are of purer eyes than to behold evil, and canst not look on iniquity" (Hab. 1:13).

While the purpose of the tabernacle was to provide a dwelling place for God among men, it was made distinctively clear that God and man could not fellowship because of the sinfulness of man and the righteousness of God. Man was barred from the presence of God because he was unfit and unholy.

In spite of the fence, man was not without hope. Thanks to a loving and merciful God, there was a gate in the fence. Although this gate will be dealt with under a separate topic, it is fitting to mention that a gate could be opened and one could find his way into the presence of God. That gate represents Jesus Christ, for He declared: "I am the way ... no man cometh to the Father, but by me"

(John 14:6). He further said: "I am the door: by me if any man enter in, he shall be saved" (John 10:9).

The only way that one could enter the gate was with an animal sacrifice. If there was no sacrifice there was no admittance. The only way we can eternally enter the presence of God is with a sacrifice. The only acceptable sacrifice to the Heavenly Father is Jesus Christ. If one appropriates Jesus Christ as his personal sacrifice, he may enter God's presence.

Even though the fence of righteousness kept the people away from the Lord, they could gain access to Him if they came in His prescribed way. This involved entering through the gate. The wall, or fence, of fine white linen represented God's perfect righteousness and said in effect: "Stay Out!" But the four-colored linen gate spoke of the mercy of God in Jesus Christ and said in effect, "Come In!"

# CHAPTER FOUR

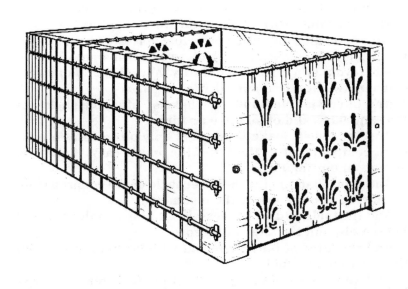

# THE BLUEPRINTS OF
# THE TABERNACLE

When they go into the tabernacle of the congregation, they shall wash with water, that they die not; or when they come near to the altar to minister, to burn offering made by fire unto the LORD:

So they shall wash their hands and their feet, that they die not: and it shall be a statute for ever to them, [even] to him and to his seed throughout their generations.

Moreover the LORD spake unto Moses, saying,

Take thou also unto thee principal spices, of pure myrrh five hundred [shekels], and of sweet cinnamon half so much, [even] two hundred and fifty [shekels], and of sweet calamus two hundred and fifty [shekels],

And of cassia five hundred [shekels], after the shekel of the sanctuary, and of oil olive an hin:

And thou shalt make it an oil of holy ointment, an ointment compound after the art of the apothecary: it shall be an holy anointing oil.

And thou shalt anoint the tabernacle of the congregation therewith, and the ark of the testimony,

And the table and all his vessels, and the candlestick and his vessels, and the altar of incense,

And the altar of burnt offering with all his vessels, and the laver and his foot.

And thou shalt sanctify them, that they may be most holy: whatsoever toucheth them shall be holy.

And thou shalt anoint Aaron and his sons, and consecrate them, that [they] may minister unto me in the priest's office.

**Exodus 30:20-30; Exodus 26:15-28; 36:31-34**

# BLUEPRINTS FOR A TABERNACLE

God's instruction to Moses was: "Let them make me a sanctuary; that I may dwell among them. According to all that I shew thee, after the pattern of the tabernacle, and the pattern of all the instruments thereof, even so shall ye make it" (Ex. 25:8-9).

In one form or another, that divine commandment was repeated again and again; for example: "Look that thou make them after their pattern, which was shewed thee in the mount" (Ex. 25:40). And again: "Moses was admonished of God when he was about to make the tabernacle: for, See, saith he, that thou make all things according to the pattern shewed to thee in the mount" (Heb. 8:5).

The only building ever constructed on this earth which was perfect from its very beginning in every detail and never again need attention, addition or alteration was the tabernacle in the wilderness. The blueprint and specifications were minutely made in Heaven. Every single detail was designed by Almighty God with every part having a prophetic, redemptive and typical significance.

From the exterior, the tabernacle was not an imposing structure and its unattractive outside gave little hint of its inner glory and beauty. A stranger viewing it from without would not have seen the exquisite beauty and the breathtaking splendor of its glorious interior.

This tabernacle now ordered of God to be set up in the wilderness, and which plan of construction was given in minute detail to Moses, was intended to be, not merely the official dwelling place of God in Israel, but a symbol, a picture and prophecy of Jesus Christ and His redemptive work. Thus, a detailed examination of the precise construction, both in design and in materials, will prove to be an exciting and profitable study.

## The Shape of the Tabernacle

There is some difference of opinion as to the shape of the tabernacle. This diversity basically is limited to the design of the roof. The traditional viewpoint is that the building proper was a flat-roofed structure with the coverings hanging over the sides and back. Some feeling this does not comply with the biblical term "tent" have developed a tabernacle that was more like a tent with ridge-poles and a sloping roof.

**The Tabernacle as Designed by James Strong**

In his book, *The Tabernacle of Israel,* James Strong maintains the tabernacle was sloped like the Bedouin and Arab tents. He goes to elaborate detail to seek to prove it was an octagonal form with perpendicular poles holding it up.

In reading his book, which is difficult in both style and in logic, it appears he is trying to prove God designed the tabernacle after the pattern of the Arab tents. He is trying to make the scriptural passage fit the design of his preconceived ideas. He has a lot of detailed description on the building of the coverings for which there is no scriptural support.

**The Tabernacle as Designed by James Ferguson**

James Ferguson's article on the tabernacle in *Smith's Bible Dictionary* has the strongest arguments favoring a pitched roof with a ridgepole. There have been some modifications by other writers who, for the most part, simplify his position.

Those holding the pitched roof, ridgepole style, argue the traditional flat roof approach does not really represent a tent. This is not a valid argument. God's design of the tabernacle was original and had nothing to do with what we traditionally think of as a tent. God did not pattern the tabernacle after any architectural design. We make a serious mistake by arguing the tabernacle had to have a certain form because it was a custom of the day.

The strongest argument most commonly presented relates to the problem of rainwater on the flat roof. Strong argued:

A flat roof would have become moldy and rotten irretrievably the first month of winter, especially with the fir robes piled on the top. Moreover, how unsightly would have been a mere box, like a coffin with a pall over it! A flat canvas roof, however tightly stretched, must have sagged so as to catch tons of water, if impervious; breaking the canvas, and indeed causing the whole structure to collapse. Of it, as is more probable, the rain would penetrate the canvas bowl, it would deluge the apartments, especially the Most Holy Place, where no one was allowed to enter, even for the purpose of lifting the roof with a rod, in order to allow the water to run off. In every point of view. The flat roof scheme is utterly impractical.

James Strong - *The Tabernacle of Israel*

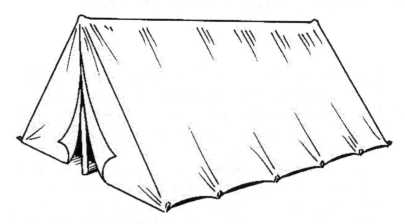

**A more simplified tabernacle with a pitched roof.**

This is a valid argument, but it is not absolutely conclusive. Even with a flat roof provisions could have been made to turn the water. The final covering was a waterproof material. Typically, it is easier to turn water with a pitched roof, but not impossible with a flat roof. There were many flat-roofed structures then as there are now.

Another argument in favor of a gable-type construction is that only one cubit of the goat's hair curtain was to hang down over the walls on each side. The basis for this argument is taken from Exodus 26:12-13. There is some debate on the meaning of this passage, and some argue that it means the goat's hair curtain only covered the sides of the tabernacle by one cubit and hung over the back by two cubits. This leaves twenty-eight cubits to be used in the pitch of the roof.

There is one major problem with this construction. Most pictures and drawings show a moderate pitch to the roof similar to modern day pitched-roof construction. Most of these have failed to calculate just how high the ridge would be if this position were correct. The following sketch shows the proportion of the pitched roof to the rest of the structure according to this position.

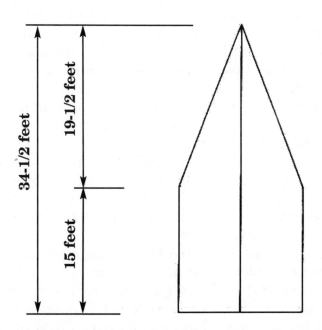

**The actual proportion to a gable-type construction.**

If we deduct the two cubits that overhang the sides, we have twenty-eight cubits on the roof. With fourteen cubits for each side, the ridge of the roof would be approximately thirteen cubits above the top of the boards. The pitched roof would be nearly five feet taller than the walls of the tabernacle. The total height would be nearly thirty-five feet, or the height of a three-and-one-half story building.

If the rain is a problem for the flat roof, consider the wind problem for such a construction. For a narrow structure forty-eight feet long and nearly thirty-five feet high, the wind load would be tremendous. This building was only held down by ropes and tent pegs. The wind would be a much greater problem to this type construction than the water would be to a flat roof.

With a ridgepole type construction, the goats' hair curtain would not be long enough to reach from the front to the rear and down the back to reach the back wall. It would be too short. Those who hold to this position just assume that it had to have a pitch and have not taken the effort to harmonize all measurements. It will not work.

The traditional viewpoint of a flat roof is probably the most popular and has the greater scriptural support. The flat-roof construction is in perfect harmony with all the measurements and structural design clearly stated in the Scripture. The most serious objection to the ridgepole type construction is that there is absolutely no mention of such in the text, nor is the existence of one even implied.

Actually, the only real argument for a pitched roof is the water problem. This position is certainly not based upon scriptural evidence requiring such construction. Even the water problem is assumed. One author found it difficult to believe that God allowed a torrential rainfall to come on His tent and upon the priests as they were offering sacrifices. There is a tradition in the writing of the ancient Hebrews that claimed it never rained on the altar. It is entirely reasonable that God controlled the elements in the immediate area of the tabernacle. And since their shoes did not wear out in the forty year journey, why would the tabernacle coverings?

## The Framework of the Tabernacle

The exact specifications for the structure of the tabernacle are found in Exodus 26:15-29 and Exodus 36:20-34.

On the exterior, the tabernacle was not anything awesome to behold. At the most, its construction might arouse curiosity. The tabernacle was an oblong building which stood on the western side of the courtyard in line with the gate. The only entrance faced the east.

The basic structure of the tabernacle consisted of vertical boards overlaid with gold with four coverings over the top. The tabernacle formed two rooms: the Holy Place and the Holy of Holies. A vail separated the two rooms. To enter the Holy Place from the outside, a hanging in the form of a curtain or vail, called the "door of the tabernacle," had to be pushed aside. To enter the Holy of Holies, the priest must pass through the first room (the Holy Place) and push aside the vail.

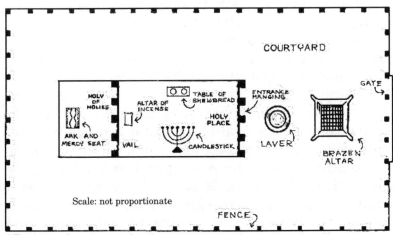

**The layout of the tabernacle.**

## The Dimensions of the Tabernacle

According to the dimensions of the boards, the tabernacle stood ten cubits (fifteen feet) high; approximately thirty cubits (forty-five feet) long; and approximately twelve cubits (eighteen feet) wide. The matter of determining the dimensions of the tabernacle may be more exact than some students are willing to admit. There are a variety of opinions as to the outside dimension.

By far, the most popular theory is that the outside dimensions of the tabernacle is thirty cubits long and ten cubits wide. Virtually, ever tabernacle writer alleges that the Holy of Holies was a cube of ten cubits, and such would require the tabernacle to be ten cubits wide. Many books go to elaborate detail to sustain the position that it was ten cubits wide on the outside dimension.

After consideration of all the evidence, this author challenges the position that the tabernacle was ten cubits wide. There is more than sufficient evidence to prove that the outside dimension of the width of the tabernacle was twelve cubits. There are three pieces of evidence that can be submitted that so prove this position.

First, let us read again Exodus 26:25: "And they shall be eight boards, and their sockets of silver, sixteen sockets." This passage is dealing with the west end of the tabernacle. When a cubit and a half, the width of each board, is multiplied by eight, the number of boards in that end, the answer would be twelve. Although there were some alterations to the corner boards for the purpose of attaching the corners, the boards were still one and one-half cubits wide, and the sockets were the same as the others.

Secondly, the Scriptures so state that the tabernacle was twelve cubits wide. Ezekiel, the prophet, gives a detailed description of the millennial temple. He stated in Ezekiel 41:1, "Afterward he brought me to the temple and measured the posts, six cubits broad on the one side, and six cubits broad on the other side, which was the breadth of the tabernacle." Six plus six equals twelve, not ten.

Thirdly, additional support for the tabernacle being twelve cubits wide is found in the goat's hair curtains. The total length of these curtains was thirty cubits (Ex.

26:8). These curtains draped over the top and down the sides. They extended nine cubits over the sides of the tabernacle to within one cubit of the ground (Ex. 26:13). If we add the length it extended over the two sides, we get eighteen cubits. Then, if we subtract the eighteen cubits from the thirty in length, we are left with twelve cubits that covered the top width of the tabernacle.

Was the Holy of Holies of the tabernacle a cube of ten cubits each direction? It would be inconsistent with all other symbols and information if it were not a cube. It was so in Solomon's temple and in the city of New Jerusalem, why not so in the tabernacle? Most authors have been so busy trying to prove the outside dimension of the tabernacle was ten cubits that they have overlooked the inside dimension. It is the interior of the tabernacle that contains the Holy of Holies, and it is the conclusion of this writer that the inter dimension of the width of the tabernacle was ten cubits. If the overall width of the tabernacle was ten cubits, and the thickness of the boards was subtracted, the interior could not be a cube. The thickness of the boards is not given. If the boards are one cubit thick, then the inside of the tabernacle had to be ten cubits wide.

There is another dimension that is only rarely considered, and that is the overall length of the tabernacle. With the west end boards overlapping the boards on the north and south sides, the overall length would be more than thirty cubits. Thirty cubits is the inside length of the tabernacle. Allowances must be made for the thickness of the boards in the back and the pillars that stood at the front entrance.

Again, the goat's hair curtains will indicate the figures with which we have to work (Ex. 26:7-13). There were eleven curtains that were four cubits wide. These were joined and made a single covering with a length of forty-four cubits. It was spread over the length of the tabernacle. One of the curtains at the front of the tabernacle was folded double. This leaves forty cubits for the goat's hair covering to cover the top length of the tabernacle and drape down the back. The curtain extended over the back to within one-half of a curtain distance (or two cubits) to the ground (Ex. 26:12). This means that eight cubits extended over the back, or west end. Subtracting the eight cubits from the forty cubits, we are left with thirty-two cubits of curtain extending across the top from the front to the rear of the tabernacle.

There is a thirty cubit distance in the twenty boards along the side. If the back boards are one cubit thick, there is a total of thirty-one cubits accounted for. If the pillars, sitting in front, are one cubit square (the same as the thickness of the walls), then there is an overall length of the tabernacle of thirty-two cubits.

When we come to the matter of the location of the vail that separates the two rooms of the tabernacle, our conclusions are reached only by deduction. We are given the location and dimensions for the vail in Solomon's temple. The two are not the same, although the proportions appear to be. If that be the case, we suppose the placing of the vail would make the Holy of Holies ten cubits square and the Holy Place ten cubits by twenty cubits.

The location of the vail is indicated by the linen and goats' hair curtains. Both of these curtains were made up of two large sections and fastened together with taches. The vail that separated the two rooms hung directly under the taches of the coverings (Ex. 26:33). Both the gold taches of the linen covering and the brass taches of the goats' hair covering lined up and lay in the same position.

If the dimensions previously stated are correct, the vail would hang exactly eleven cubits from the back wall. The vail hung on pillars that were one cubit thick. This construction left the inside of the Holy of Holies ten cubits from top to bottom, from side to side, and from the back of the pillars to the back wall. The Holy of Holies was exactly a cube.

## The Boards of the Tabernacle

Detailed instructions for the boards are found in Exodus 36:20-30 and Exodus 26:15-15

The tabernacle walls were made of boards of shittim (acacia) wood and overlaid with gold. These boards stood ten cubits (fifteen feet), and were one and one-half cubits (twenty-seven inches) wide. In keeping with the overall dimensions of the tabernacle, it is concluded the boards were one cubit (eighteen inches) thick. The boards stood vertically to form the walls. Underneath each board was two "tenons," probably a dowel, which was set into the silver bases to hold the boards stationary at the bottom.

The verses pertaining to the corner boards are of difficult interpretation. A passage relating to this is found in Exodus 26:23-25:

> And two boards shalt thou make for the corners of the tabernacle in the two sides.
>
> And they shall be coupled together beneath, and they shall be coupled together above the head of it unto one ring: thus shall it be for them both; they shall be for the two corners.
>
> And they shall be eight boards, and their sockets [of] silver, sixteen sockets; two sockets under one board, and two sockets under another board.

Opinions regarding these corner boards are diversified. But when all has been stated, there is still no reason to believe that these corner boards are any different than the others in shape and size. They are listed with the other, and they each have the two sockets of silver of the same weight as the other boards. There was some type of ring or staple used to attach them to the boards of the north and south sides. Probably, the only significance to these attaching devices was merely to add strength to the whole structure and connect the sides and the end together. The material used to make them is not given, but they had to be one of the materials given for the construction, probably gold.

The twofold material in the boards is a symbol of the twofold nature of Jesus Christ. As the board was of two materials, He was of two natures: the nature of man, and the nature of God.

The wood is a symbol of His human nature. He was "found in fashion as a man" (Phil. 2:8). "But when the fullness of time was come, God sent forth his Son, made of a woman, made under the law" (Gal. 4:4). Jesus took upon Himself the form of a man and became subject to it and its nature, to the degree He "was in all points tempted like as we are, yet without sin" (Heb. 4:15).

The gold overlaying the boards symbolizes His divine nature. The gold being a bright yellowish color represents the glory of God. "In him dwelleth all the fullness of the Godhead bodily" (Col. 2:9). He is our "great God and our Saviour Jesus Christ" (Titus 2:13).

The total weight of the gold donated was twenty-nine talents, and seven-hundred-thirty shekels (Ex. 38:24). The market value of the pure gold at $407.00 per troy ounce is $1,623,930.00. (Figured at: one talent equals one hundred-twenty-five pounds troy weight, twelve ounces equals one pound troy weight, two shekels equals one ounce troy weight).

The two materials, the incorruptible wood and the gold, constitute not two, but one board of the tabernacle. The two materials were absolutely distinct. The wood never became gold and the gold never became wood. The two natures in Christ are distinct. His humanity never becomes deity, and His deity never merges into His humanity. They were absolutely distinct and separate from each other. But while the two natures dwelt in Him and were distinct. He was not two persons but one; nevertheless, He was personally God and personally man. It is a mystery beyond human solution how the two distinct natures could be united in the one person so that the two natures were never confounded nor the personality divided.

## The Bars

The instructions for constructing the bars are found in Exodus 36:31-34 and Exodus 26:26-29.

On the three sides of the tabernacle, the boards standing upright were held together by means of bars. These bars were made of the same wood as the boards and overlaid with gold. There were golden rings in the boards through which these bars would pass and hold the boards together. Five bars were used on each side to hold the boards together.

There is lack of sufficient detail to determine exactly how these bars were placed on the boards. The difficulty arises from an interpretation of Exodus 36:33 which says: "And he made the middle bar to shoot through the boards from the one end to the other."

Some understanding this to mean that there are three rows of the bars on each side. This makes for two short bars at the top each extending half way; one bar tin the middle that extends the full length of the side; and two short bars at the bottom that also extend half way.

Others understand this to mean that there are five rows of bars. They claim that there are four rows of bars on the outside surface extending the full length of the sides and then a fifth bar running through the inside of the boards the full length of the tabernacle.

Either of these positions is possible, although there are those who take one or the other position and argue that the other will not work. There is no passage that denies that all the bars do not run the full length. The boards were eighteen inches thick and it is entirely possible that the middle bar ran through the inside of the boards. How the bars were placed is not particularly significant, or else the Lord would have given us more exact information. It only matters if one is going to build a scale model, and then he can do it either way.

The spiritual significance of the materials of the bars is the same as that of the boards. The wood represents Christ as a man, and the gold represents Christ as God. As in the boards, the combination of the two reveal His incarnation.

The fact that the bars held the building together may have spiritual significance within itself. As the creator, all things exist and are held together by Jesus Christ. "In the beginning was the Word, and the Word was with God, and the Word was God. The same was in the beginning with God. All things were made by him; and without him was not anything made that was made. And the Word was made flesh, and dwelt (tabernacled) among us, (and we beheld his glory, the glory as of the only begotten of the Father,) full of grace and truth" (John 1:1-3, 14). "And he is before all things, and by him all things consist (are held together)" (Col. 1:17).

## The Silver Foundation

The tabernacle is the only building ever erected having a foundation made of pure silver. The forty-eight boards rested on ninety-six blocks of silver weighing about one hundred pounds each. The four pillars holding the vail also had silver bases weighing about one hundred pounds each. This made a combined weight of pure silver for the bases to be ten thousand pounds or five tons.

The instructions for the foundation are stated in Exodus 38:27 which states: "And of the hundred talents of silver were cast the sockets of the sanctuary, and the sockets of the vail; an hundred sockets of the hundred talents, a talent for a socket."

These blocks of silver were placed upon the desert ground, the upright boards were placed on the sockets of silver with their tenons fitting snugly into the foundation. The exact shape and fashion of these sockets are not given. The sockets underneath the pillars were the same weight as those under the boards. Only one socket was required under each pillar.

The silver was not one of the voluntary gifts for its erection. The silver furnished for these sockets was the silver collected each time a census was taken. Silver amounting to a half shekel was required from each male, twenty years and upward each time a census was taken (Ex. 30:11-17). This money was called "ransom" or "atonement" money. The purpose of the half shekel being collected at the numbering of the men is stated in Exodus 30:12, "that there be no plague among them, when thou numberest them." This plague was symbolic of the penalty or wages of sin - death.

Each man was required to give an offering to the Lord in the amount of half a shekel after the shekel of the sanctuary. The rich were not allowed to give more and the poor could not give less. The amount was fixed and could not be changed for any reason. The price was the same for all.

The total amount collected from the redemption money was one hundred talents, and 1,775 shekels (Ex. 38:25). Of this, the one hundred talents were used for the bases of the boards and pillars, and the rest were used for all the other silver items. The total weight of the silver exceeded six tons. The market value of the pure silver at $6.62 per troy ounce would be about $1,000,000.00. (Figured at: one talent equals one hundred twenty-five pounds troy weight. Twelve ounces equals one pound troy weight. Two shekels equals one ounce.)

The fact that the silver came from the atonement money indicates, without question, that silver pictures redemption.

The silver money is a symbol of the precious price paid by our Lord Jesus Christ for the ransom of the saved; as it is written: "Ye are bought with a price (1 Cor. 6:20).

The silver is symbolic. It is symbolic of the true price paid for the redemption of the souls of man. "Ye were not redeemed with corruptible things, as silver and gold ... but with the precious blood of Christ, as of a lamb without blemish and without spot" (1 Peter 1:18-19). The word "precious" means "costly." It cost Christ His blood, the greatest price ever paid for anything, ever!

It might seem to be a little strange, but the cost of our redemption was the only price God had to pay for anything. When He wants something He just creates it. When He wanted a world, He just spoke and there it was. If He wants more gold and silver and precious jewels, He can just create more. One day He will speak again and create a new Heaven and earth. But when it came to our redemption, God had to buy that. It was the only thing God ever bought, and the price paid for it was the greatest price ever paid for anything.

Jesus testified: "Even as the Son of man came not to be ministered unto, but to minister, and to give his life a ransom for many" (Matt. 20:28). And Paul said of Christ: "Who gave himself a ransom for all" (1 Tim. 2:6). Sin is stealing against the character and the righteousness of God. When one steals, he takes away from another that which is rightfully his. Man was commanded from the beginning to give honor and glory to God. When he sins, he robs God of the honor and glory due Him. Man is not capable of paying God for that which he has stolen from Him. God is the only person capable of paying man's great debt of sin. Since the wages of sin is death, God gave His only begotten Son, literally Himself, as payment for man's sin. Silver is only a symbol of that great payment of atonement made from Heaven.

The equal payment on the part of each man indicates the redemptive price for each person is the same. The payment for the sins of man by Christ on the cross was the same for every man. A half shekel is worth about $1.75. All could afford it; none were too poor. Rich man, poor man, good man, mean man; the price for his salvation is the same as for every other man.

It was the men who were "twenty years old and above" that were numbered and had to pay the half shekel "ransom for his soul unto the Lord." This age was the age of marriage; the age when the men were husbands and fathers. The sin nature is passed from generation to generation by the father. Perhaps there is some significance of only the men and fathers having to pay the redemption token, inasmuch as they were responsible for the transmission of sin.

Jesus died to pay the cost to redeem the sin nature of all mankind. First, John 2:2: "And he is the propitiation for our sins: and not for our's only, but also for the sins of the whole world." Men do not go to hell because they inherited their sin nature. The payment for their sin nature has been paid whether they know it or not; hence, the children who die in infancy are covered by the blood and enter Heaven. Men go to hell because they knowingly and willingly sin and do not seek forgiveness. Granted, their sin nature leads them to sin, but the sin nature they inherited has been redeemed for all men.

All men, saved and lost, have benefited from the death of Christ. But when one sins knowingly and willingly, he becomes responsible for his personal behavior and must then seek God's forgiveness and mercy for his actions. In doing so, the blood of Christ covers these sins. In failing to do so, he perishes by his own choice and pays the price for his own sins. But a man will not suffer in hell because of his inherited sin nature, only indirectly as his sin nature influences him to sin, and for that he must seek forgiveness.

Each time a census was taken of the man, the half shekel had to be collected to prevent a plague. King David took a census against good advice and 70,000 men died (2 Samuel 24:1-17). Many things were involved in this situation, but one of them was the failure to collect the half shekel of silver. Israel's failure to collect the atonement money was a symbolic declaration that there was no sin nature and no need of redemption and salvation from sins. Such kindled the anger of God, and God taught Israel by the plague that there was sin in the people and that sin brings death. If God deals thusly with those who tamper with the symbolisms of salvation, woe be unto those who tamper with the plan of salvation.

## The Pillars

There were three sets of pillars. Sixty pillars of the court fence surrounded the tabernacle. Four of these pillars constituted the entrance into the courtyard. Five pillars were at the eastern end of the tabernacle which formed the door into it. Four pillars were inside the tabernacle between the Holy Place and the Holy of Holies.

The spiritual symbolism in the entrances is not so much in the pillars themselves, as in the hangings mounted on the pillars. If it can be found, there might be some importance associated with the style and the number of pillars.

The four pillars at the eastern end of the courtyard constituted the gate or entrance into the courtyard area (Ex. 27:16-17). These four pillars were the same as the other pillars holding up the fence of fine twined linen. No material was listed in the making of these pillars, but it is concluded since the others were of acacia (shittim) wood that they too were made of the same. These pillars were set in bases of brass and had caps of silver at the top. Like the fence, they were stabilized by means of cords and stakes.

The five pillars at the eastern end of the tabernacle constituted the gate or entrance into the sanctuary. These five pillars were made of acacia wood and were covered with gold. Standing on brass bases, they were topped with capitals of gold. The rods or fillets on which the entrance vail hung were also covered in gold. Exodus 36:38 gives the instructions: "And the five pillars of it with their hooks; and he overlaid their chapiters and their fillets with gold: but their five sockets were of brass."

The exact size of these pillars is not given. We assume them to be equal to the height of the tabernacle at ten cubits. The top of these pillars had "chapiters" or crown like decorations of gold. This leads us to believe that this aspect of the work of Christ is that of a king or judge.

The four pillars in the inside of the tabernacle separate the Holy Place from the Holy of Holies and it was the door or entrance into the Holy of Holies. The instruction for their construction is found in Exodus 36:36: "And he made thereunto four pillars of shittim wood, and overlaid them with gold: their hooks were of gold; and he cast for them four sockets of silver."

These pillars were of a more simple construction. No chapiters were on top. The height is assumed to be ten cubits. They sat on sockets or bases of silver. The sockets under each pillar were the same weight as the sockets under the boards, that is one talent (Ex. 38:27). There were two sockets under each board and only one under each pillar. This might suggest something of the size of the pillar. Most designers show the post to be one cubit square, which would be slightly more than one-half the size of the boards. No one really knows whether any of the pillars were round or square and there is no way of actually proving either. Square pillars seem to fit the architectural design of the tabernacle better and most everyone simply considers them to be square.

Whatever spiritual significance might be given to the pillars is purely speculation on the part of the author. The Scriptures give no hint of any symbolical significance. There is most likely some significance because of the number of pillars and their design. The five pillars at the entrance to the tabernacle and the four pillars at the entrance to the Holy of Holies did not have that numerical

requirement because the structure required it. Each pillar was likely eighteen inches square. Between the five
pillars at the entrance to the tabernacle was only a distance of about thirty-one and one-half inches. Between
the four pillars at the entrance into the Holy of Holies was
only a distance of about thirty-six inches.

The pillars entering the tabernacle had a gold crown
at the top and were set in brass bases. The pillars entering the Holy of Holies had no crown at the top and were
set in silver bases. The pillars in the courtyard had silver
tops and brass bases. There had to be more of a spiritual
significance behind the build and design of these pillars
than merely a structural requirement. Needless to say,
many authors have stated their opinions, but some of
them have crossed the border into becoming ridiculous.
No author can write with certainty the meaning of the
tabernacle pillars.

One writer claims the four pillars at the entrance to
the courtyard illustrate the fourfold Sonship of Jesus
Christ. He was the Son of David, the Son of Abraham, Son
of man and the Son of God. As the Son of David, He is the
heir of David's throne and ordained to sit upon it (Luke
1:32). As the son of Abraham, He is the Seed promised to
Abraham (Gal. 3:16). As the Son of man, He is the final
judge (Acts 17:31). And as the Son of God, He is the
Father's heir of all things (Heb. 1:2).

Another author claims the five pillars at the entrance
to the tabernacle represent the five titles of Christ in
Isaiah 9:6. These five titles are: Wonderful, Counselor,
The mighty God, The everlasting Father and the Prince of
Peace. The crown like decorations of gold at the top at
least can find similarity in these titles.

On the four pillars entering the Holy of Holies hung
the vail. The vail is declared to represent the life of Jesus
Christ (Heb. 10:19-20). It has been suggested that these
pillars possibly support the premise that Christ was
incarnate God in man. They would be the strength and

evidence of the identity of Christ. These four pillars could well represent the birth, life, death and resurrection of Jesus Christ. All were miraculous and stand as the witness and the evidence that Jesus was God in flesh. The fact that these pillars had no crowns explains the fact that Christ first came in human flesh as Savior and not as King.

## The Pins and Cords

The courtyard fence and the tabernacle were secured by means of pins and cords. The pins were made of brass and the cods were made of linen since the only material in the tabernacle was linen. "And all the pins of the tabernacle, and of the court round about, were of brass" (Ex. 38:20).

Each pillar of the fence was secured by two cords tied to the pillar and each attached to a pin, one of which was on the inside of the fence and the other on the outside. The Merarites handled the court pins and cords (Num. 3:33-37; 4:29-32).

We are told the tabernacle was secured by the pins and cords, but we do not know exactly how. Almost all scale models and drawings show the rams' skins and badgers' skins pulled down by means of the cords. This is entirely likely because no size or specifics are given for these coverings as there is for the linen and goats' hair coverings. There were definitely pins and cords for the tabernacle, and in the least the cords were pulled tight over the tabernacle. The Gershonites handled these coverings and the cords to the tabernacle (Num. 3:25026; 4:24-26).

The pens were made of copper or brass. These tent pins are also called "nails" in the Bible. In other places they are called "stakes." In a direct reference in Isaiah 22:23, Christ is compared to a nail: "And I will fasten him as a nail in a sure place; and he shall be for a glorious throne to his father's house."

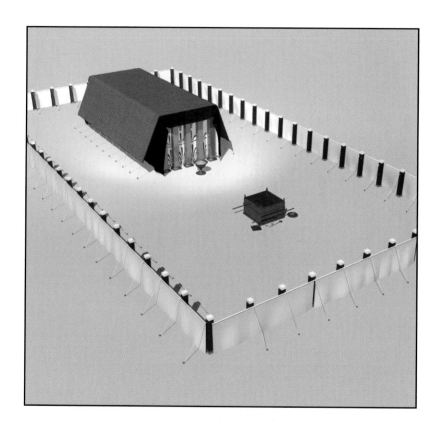

# Digital Renderings
## of the Tabernacle

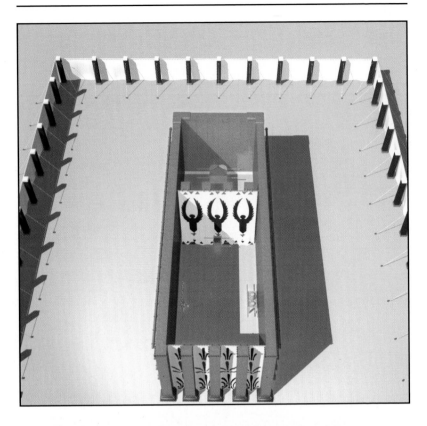

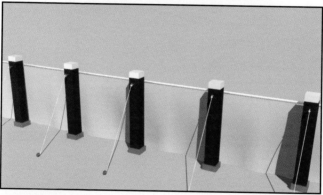

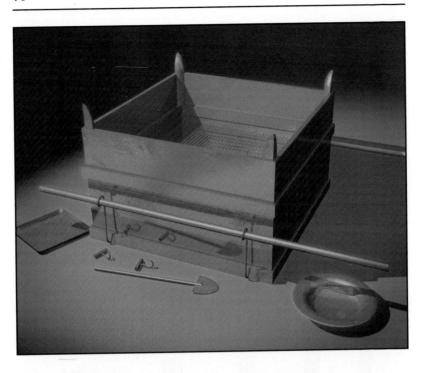

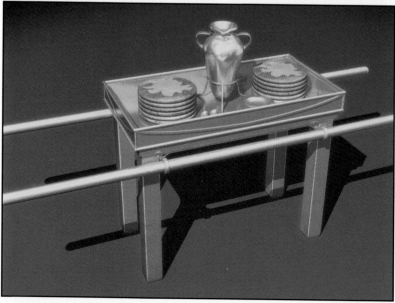

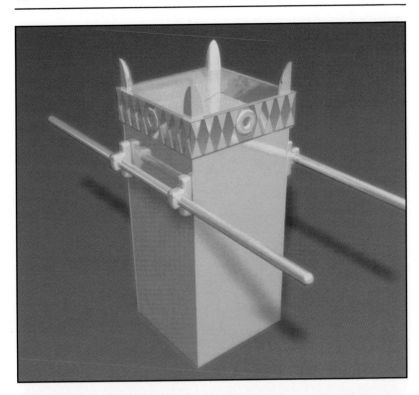

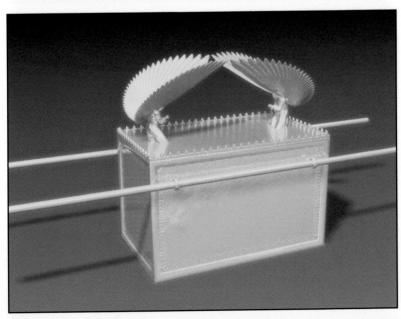

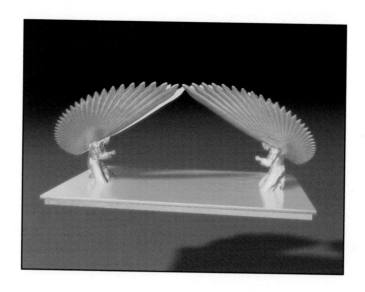

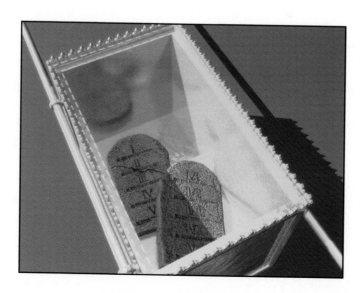

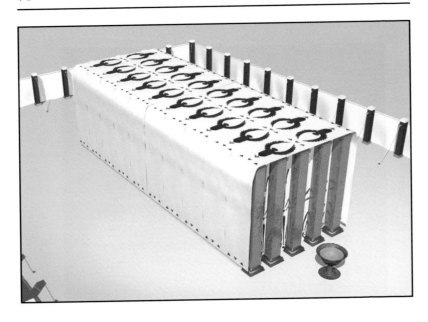

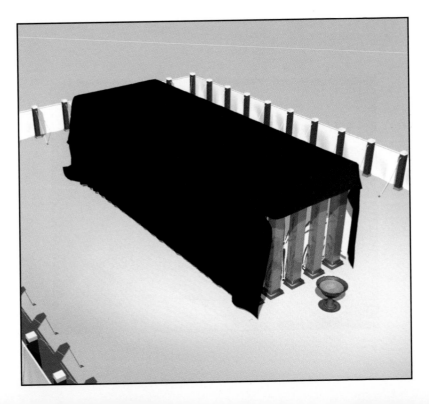

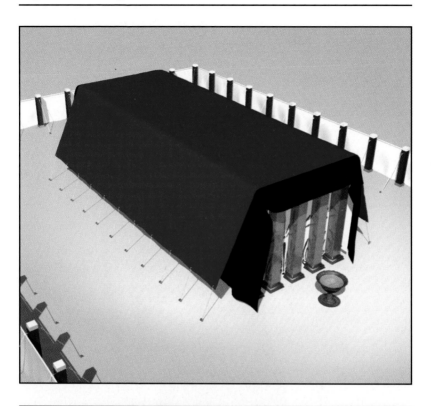

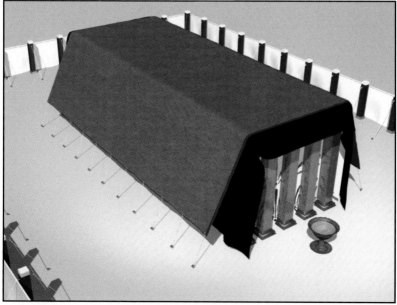

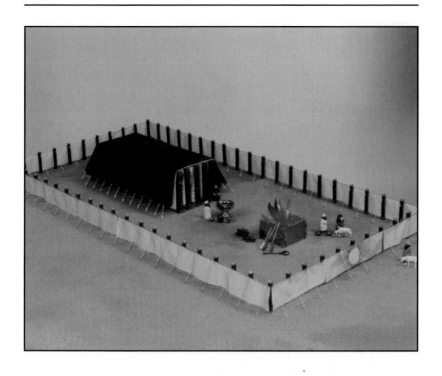

**Pictures of the original scale model of the tabernacle built by Dr. Bobby L. Sparks. The scale model was appraised at $20,000.00.**

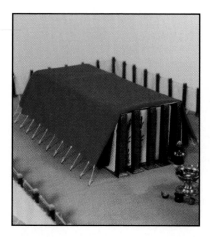

# CHAPTER FIVE

# THE COVERINGS OF THE
# TABERNACLE

And thou shalt make curtains [of] goats' [hair] to be a covering upon the tabernacle: eleven curtains shalt thou make.

The length of one curtain [shall be] thirty cubits, and the breadth of one curtain four cubits: and the eleven curtains [shall be all] of one measure.

And thou shalt couple five curtains by themselves, and six curtains by themselves, and shalt double the sixth curtain in the forefront of the tabernacle.

And thou shalt make fifty loops on the edge of the one curtain [that is] outmost in the coupling, and fifty loops in the edge of the curtain which coupleth the second.

And thou shalt make fifty taches of brass, and put the taches into the loops, and couple the tent together, that it may be one.

And the remnant that remaineth of the curtains of the tent, the half curtain that remaineth, shall hang over the backside of the tabernacle.

And a cubit on the one side, and a cubit on the other side of that which remaineth in the length of the curtains of the tent, it shall hang over the sides of the tabernacle on this side and on that side, to cover it.

And thou shalt make a covering for the tent [of] rams' skins dyed red, and a covering above [of] badgers' skins.

**Exodus 26:7-14; Cf. Exodus 36:8-18**

# THE COVERINGS OF THE TABERNACLE

The tabernacle did not have any solid ceilings as is customary in our houses. The roof of the tabernacle consisted of four layers of materials. In the King James Version, these coverings are called "curtains." To our way of reckoning, we call them coverings and this is the term that will be used throughout this study.

Several authors and artists have the concept that the tabernacle had a pitched configuration. One author maintained that the Bedouin tribes in the wilderness areas always had pitched roofs to their tents so the tabernacle likewise must have had a pitched roof. The author forgets that the Bedouins did not design the tabernacle, God did. There is absolutely no provision for the tabernacle to have a pitched roof.

After the Lord confronted Adam and Eve about their sins, He covered their nakedness with a covering of animal skins. Over the tabernacle, there are a series of coverings. These coverings likewise have spiritual significance indicating the provision of the coverings the Lord has made for sinners. The first covering was a linen curtain. The second was a covering of goats' hair. The third was a covering of rams' skins that were dyed red. And the fourth was a covering of badgers' skins. An independent inquiry of each covering is very significant.

## The Linen Covering

The first covering to go over the tabernacle was the linen covering (Ex. 26:1-6: 36:8-13).

In all, ten single linen curtains were made. Each covering was six feet (four cubits) wide by forty-two feet (twenty-eight cubits) long. Five of these were fastened together (probably with needle work) in one group to make one broad covering. There were now two broad linen coverings, each thirty feet (twenty cubits) wide and forty-two feet (twenty-eight cubits) long. On one edge of each of these two broad curtains was sewn loops of blue. Then fifty gold taches, or clasps, were used to join together the two broad curtains with the loops of blue. This made one curtain called one tabernacle, and measured sixty feet (forty cubits) by forty-two feet (twenty-eight cubits). The total length of the ten curtains equaled 280 cubits, which was exactly the length of the linen fence.

The gold taches fastening the two broad curtains together reached across the top of the tabernacle thirty feet (twenty cubits) back from the front entrance. The vail was hung immediately under the taches (Ex. 26:33). This gives the location of the vail and the approximate dimensions of the two rooms. The Holy Place was fifteen feet wide (ten cubits) by thirty feet (twenty cubits), and the Holy of Holies was fifteen feet (ten cubits) square.

This curtain was made of "fine twined linen" which was very white in color. Cherubim were embroidered on these coverings in colors of blue, purple and scarlet. The word for embroidered is a word that means the emblem was actually woven into the fabric rather than stitched on the surface. The basic color of this covering was white with images of angelic creatures woven into it in colors of blue purple and scarlet.

In the ancient Hebrew language there is no specific words for color. When a color is given, the Hebrew word is literally the name of the source from which the color comes from. For instance, the word scarlet is the name of a worm in the larva stage. Red dye is extracted from the worm. In the case of the blue dye, the Hebrew word is the name of a snail like shellfish that is found in the Mediterranean Sea. The blue dye indicates something of the expensiveness of the tabernacle because one source required approximately 250,000 shellfish to make one ounce of blue dye.

The colors of the linen covering are significant. This linen curtain represented Christ in all of His glory and perfect righteousness. The red scarlet color represents the blood of Christ shed for our sins. The blue is the color of heaven and indicates that our Savior came from heaven and not the earth. The purple color is the color of royalty and lets us know that it was the King on the throne of Heaven that paid the price of our salvation. The white linen covering was a righteous covering for the sinner. In the Book of Revelation, the bride is said to be arrayed in "fine linen, clean and white, which is the righteousness of the saints." Where did the saints get that righteous dress? They did not earn it. It was imputed to them by Christ.

If we are going to fellowship with God, we have to be righteous. We cannot obtain that kind of righteousness by our own works, but Jesus will impute His righteousness into us and clothe us in His holiness.

The priest who walked beneath these curtains walked beneath a mass of outspread wings of cherubim. As the priests ministered in the tabernacle and looked upward, they saw the cherubim and were reminded that God was constantly watching over them. In the Bible, cherubim are always seen as guardians of the holiness of God. The priests were constantly reminded of God's presence. We do well indeed if we continually keep this fact before us. It will cause us to conduct ourselves in a manner pleasing to God and becoming to us.

## The Goats' Hair Covering

The second covering to go over the tabernacle was placed directly on top of the linen covering (Ex. 26:7-13; 36:14-18). There were eleven curtains in the tabernacle made of goats' hair. Each curtain was six feet (four cubits) wide by forty-five feet (thirty cubits) long.

Five of these were fastened together to make one broad curtain and six were fastened together to make the second broad curtain. The two broad goats' hair curtains were then coupled together by means of fifty brass clasps. The loops in which the clasps were attached were not named in color. This made one large covering that measured forty-five feet (thirty cubits) by sixty-six feet (forty-four cubits).

Of the broad front section containing six of the curtains, the sixth curtain is said to be doubled in the forefront of the tabernacle. Does this curtain hang double over the front of the tabernacle? Or does this curtain lie over another curtain in the very front of the tabernacle to create a double layer? The language permits either, and the tabernacle designers have designed both. The significance of this doubled curtain is not known.

The "cubit on the side which remaineth in the length of the curtains" has universally been interpreted to mean that after the curtain was stretched over the walls of the tabernacle that it lacked one cubit on each side reaching the ground. This is definitely the case when the length of the curtains are subtracted from the dimensions of the tabernacle with a flat roof. However, there are those who understand it to mean that the curtain only covered the walls by one cubit. This is the strongest argument in favor of a ridgepole, pitched-roof structure. If only one cubit of the curtain covers the sides, then there remains twenty-eight cubits for the pitch of the roof. Such an amount would require that the pitched roof be much taller than the tabernacle itself. This position just has too many problems.

The goats' hair curtain hung over the rear of the tabernacle to within two cubits of the ground. "And the remnant that remaineth... shall hang over the backside of the tabernacle" (verse 12). Instead of saying two cubits remained, it said that half a curtain remained. This arrangement is in exact harmony with the other given dimensions of the tabernacle. And again, a hangover of two cubits on the back would be utterly impossible with a pitched roof. Matter of fact, the curtain would not even reach the top of the wall from the top of the ridge.

The goats' hair curtain lay in the exact same position on the tabernacle that the linen curtain did. The fifty taches of brass were in line with the fifty taches of gold, and the vail hung directly under both. The only difference was that the goats' hair curtain was one cubit longer than the linen curtain on each side, and it was doubled over in the front. Draping over the back, the linen and goats' hair curtains were the same length.

The curtain was not made of goats' skins. It was made of goats' hair. However, the word "hair" is not in the text. Had the "skins" of goats been intended, that word would doubtless have been used, as in the description of the two outer coverings of rams skins and badgers' skins (Ex. 26:14). There may be several reasons why the word "hair" is omitted. First, it may be that our attention is more closely called to the goats and the significance of the animals. Secondly, the chief word for "hair" is derived from the same root as the word for goat; though there are two words for goat, one meaning "a hairy one" and the other, used here, meaning "a strong one."

When the list is given for the materials and talents donated for use in building the tabernacle, the women are said to have "spun goats' hair." Again the word "hair" is omitted, but only the hair could be spun.

Just what color was these goats' hair coverings? Black! Nearly all models and pictures of the tabernacle from our part of the world show the goats' hair covering to be an off white or grayish color. This is the typical color of the goats in our area, but the goats in the middle eastern countries are black. The tabernacle was built in a country where a white goat is a rarity. White goats have been imported into that area. Many have concluded that because goats' hair is white in the western world, that this covering was white. Black is a far more fitting color. A goat was mostly used as a sin-offering. Black is the emblematic color of sin.

This covering made of goats' hair represents Jesus Christ as the sin-offering. The goat is mentioned in connection with the sin-offering and sinners. We read: "Take ye a kid of the goats for a sin-offering" (Lev. 9:3; Cf. Nun. 28:15). "Take. . . two kids of the goats for a sin-offering" on the great Day of Atonement (Lev. 16:5-28). "He shall separate them one from another, as a shepherd divideth his sheep from the goats" - representing the saved and the unsaved at the Judgment of the Nations (Matt. 25:32).

Numerous passages clearly state that Christ was literally the sin-offering for mankind. "It pleased the LORD to bruise him; he hath put him to grief: when thou shalt make his soul an offering for sin" (Isa. 53:10). "In the end of the world (age) hath he appeared to put away sin by the sacrifice of himself" (Heb. 9:26). "Christ was once offered to bear the sins of many" (Heb. 9:28). He hath made him to be sin for us" (2 Cor. 5:21). "Christ also hath loved us, and hath given himself for us an offering" (Eph. 5:2).

One last feature must be noted: the two sets of goats' hair curtains were fastened together by fifty taches of brass. The brass represents Christ suffering our judgment for us. With the taches and the hair, we have a double feature in the representation of Christ bearing the penalty of our sins.

## Rams' Skins Dyed Red Covering

In this covering, we have quite an absence of detail and the attention is directed to only a few features. The brief details are stated in Exodus 26:14: "And thou shalt make a covering for the tent of rams' skins dyed red (Cf. Ex. 36:19). These words give us three features to be dealt with: the animals were rams; their skins were used; and these were dyed red.

We do not know the exact size or shape of it, and we can not positively prove how it was attached. In the instructions given to the family of Levites in charge of setting up and taking down the tabernacle reference is made to the brass nails associated with the tabernacle building. Most model builders show this covering pulled over the top, and with linen cords pulled tightly and tied to the brass nails serving as tent pegs. This is the position that just about every artist and model builder has come to accept. The lack of a specific size and the presence of the tent pegs would seem to indicate this possibility.

This arrangement would also provide other possibilities. With the building being fifteen feet (10 cubits) high and the covering pulled over the side at an angle and tied to the brass nails, this would leave an area immediately next to the outside wall that could be used as a utility area. It does not have specific spiritual significance, so no mention is made of it. There would have been need for such a storage place somewhere in the precincts of the sanctuary to keep the holy vessels, and so on.

The rams' skins pointed to the Lord Jesus Christ in the role of a substitute for sinners. It speaks of the substitutionary atonement made by the blood of the Lord Jesus Christ in our behalf. The color red, as it occurs in the tabernacle, invariably speaks of the blood of the Lord and the atonement which He made for sins. The skins, of course, speak of the complete covering of sin for the sinner. The substitute must give its blood before the sinner can be clothed by the covering of this substitute.

The ram is set before us in Scripture as a substitute. When Abraham lifted up his knife to slay his son as a sacrificial offering unto the Lord, the voice of the angel of the Lord prevented him from doing so. When at that command, he turned away from the altar, he beheld a ram caught by its horns in a thicket. And then we are told: "And Abraham went and took the ram, and offered him up for a burnt offering in the stead of his son" (Gen.

22:13). Notice the words: "in the stead (or place) of his son." Abraham realized that it was a picture of the coming substitute, the Lord Jesus Christ. This is implied in the words of Abraham: "And Abraham called the name of that place Jehovah-jireh (JEHOVAH will provide a substitute for me): as it is said to this day, In the mount of the LORD it shall be seen" (Gen. 22:14). The fact that Abraham spoke in the future tense indicates that the mount of which he spoke is most likely Mount Calvary.

The Lord Jesus Christ came into the world to be a substitute for guilty sinners. He came to take the place of condemned men and women. He came to exchange places with those who were under the sentence of death. He came into the world to trade places with the sinner condemned to death and eternal banishment from God. He came to take the place of those who justly should suffer the downpour of the righteous wrath of the righteous God for ever.

Is there any thing more clearly set forth in Scripture than this concerning our Lord Jesus Christ? "His own self bear our sins in his own body on the tree" (1 Peter 2:24). "Christ died for our sins according to the scriptures" (1 Cor. 15:3). "Who gave himself for our sins" (Gal. 1:4). "Who was delivered for our offenses" (Rom. 4:25). "The LORD hath laid on him the iniquity of us all" (Isa. 53:6).

## The Badgers' Skin Covering

We come now to the fourth and outer covering of the tabernacle. The record is very brief: And thou shalt make a covering for the tent of rams' skins dyed red, and a covering above of badgers' skins" (Ex. 26:14).

Before much else can be said about this covering, it must be established exactly what this covering was, In the King James translation we have the word "badger," but there is some concern as to what this animal really was. It was not likely what we westerners call a badger. A badger as we know it is not found in that area of the world. The Hebrew word itself refers to some kind of marine animal. The most likely animal and by far the most popular animal used would have been the dugong found in the Mediterranean Sea. Since that kind of animal is not found in most costal waters of other places in the world it is unfamiliar to most people. However, the dugong was plentiful in the Mediterranean Sea at that time and was commonly used for waterproof and other leather applications. An adult dugong is ten feet long and its skin was the standard material for making sandals in the East Sinai peninsula. It is likely that the folk in Great Britain, the same folk, who translated the King James Version, were familiar with the animal and it could have been a common title that they designated to the dugong. We do not know why they used that term, but it is not important as long as we know what kind of animal it was.

As in the rams' skins covering, the size, shape and means of attaching this covering are not known. And, we can only assume with the presence of the brass tent nails that this covering was tied down by means of linen cords and attached to those nails.

Since we cannot be absolutely exact about the animal we cannot be certain about the color of the skins. But since the possible animal selections may have similarity of color, the color may be a dull bluish gray or brown. These skins had no colorful beauty, not repulsive in appearance, but not particularly attractive. It was the only covering visible to the outsider, and gave little hint of the beauty beneath the drab exterior.

Trying to determine the significance of this last and final covering over the tabernacle is not so easy. If this covering had any significance other than protecting the top of the tabernacle, it would certainly represent Jesus Christ as He appeared in the eyes of men. As viewed by the unbeliever, there was nothing attractive in Jesus Christ. Isaiah prophesied of Him: "He hath no form nor comeliness; and when we shall see him, there is no beauty that we should desire him. He is despised and rejected of men; a man of sorrows, and acquainted with grief: and we hid as it were our faces from him; he was despised, and we esteemed him not" (Isa. 53:2-3). Had we seen Jesus walking across the hillside of Galilee, we would not have recognized Him as the Son of God. He appeared in the eyes of men as an ordinary person.

No one who saw the tabernacle under the outer covering of badgers' skins would have dreamed of the wealth, the gold, the form, the color and the exquisite beauty beneath it. Just as a person had to come to the inside of the tabernacle to see its beauty, a person needs to receive Jesus

Christ as Savior and thus enter into fellowship with Him in order to fully appreciate the beauty of His holiness.

# CHAPTER SIX

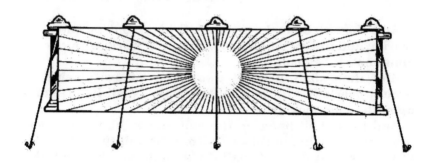

# THE CURTAINS OF THE
# TABERNACLE

And the hanging for the gate of the court [was] needle-work, [of] blue, and purple, and scarlet, and fine twined linen: and twenty cubits [was] the length, and the height in the breadth [was] five cubits, answerable to the hangings of the court.

Exodus 38:18; Cf. Exodus 27:16

And thou shalt make an hanging for the door of the tent, [of] blue, and purple, and scarlet, and fine twined linen, wrought with needlework.

Exodus 26:36; Cf. Exodus 36:37

And thou shalt make a vail [of] blue, and purple, and scarlet, and fine twined linen of cunning work: with cherubims shall it be made:

And thou shalt hang it upon four pillars of shittim [wood] overlaid with gold: their hooks [shall be of] gold, upon the four sockets of silver.

And thou shalt hang up the vail under the taches, that thou mayest bring in thither within the vail the ark of the testimony: and the vail shall divide unto you between the holy [place] and the most holy.

Exodus 26:31-33; Cf. Exodus 36:35-36

# THE CURTAINS OF THE TABERNACLE

The word "hanging" is applied exclusively to three special curtains: the one at the gate of the court; the one at the entrance to the tabernacle; and the third which hung between the Holy Place and the Most Holy Place. This third curtain was designated as the "vail."

The word "hanging" is translated from a Hebrew word with a variety of meanings: "to conceal, cover, protect, to shut in, confine, booth, tent, etc." In the context of the tabernacle, these hangings served as a gate, a door or an entrance way. They protected the holiness of God, who was inside. The unrighteousness of mankind was confined to the exterior, not being allowed to enter in.

All three of the hangings were made of the same material and arranged in precisely the same order: "blue, and purple, and scarlet, and fine twined linen." There was a difference between the vail and the others, as the vail had cherubim embroidered on it. All three were of the same dimension as regards their area which was one hundred cubits. The gate of the court was five by twenty cubits equaling one hundred square cubits. The entrance and vail each occupied a space of ten cubits by ten cubits or a hundred square cubits each.

## The Curtain That Hung On the Gate of the Courtyard

The gate faced east, the direction of the rising sun. It was twenty cubits or thirty feet wide, and five cubits or seven and one-half feet high. No details are given as how the colors of blue, purple and scarlet were embroidered into fine twined linen. It was held up by the strength of four pillars.

The pure linen fence, which represented the righteousness of the Lord Jesus Christ, was of one color. But the
gate had four colors - blue, purple, scarlet and white.
White linen symbolizes righteousness and the perfect
character of the Lord. Blue is the color of Heaven and
speaks of Christ's heavenly character. Purple, the color
associated with royalty, pointed to Jesus Christ as the
king and supreme over all. Scarlet, or red, is the color of
blood and looks ahead to Jesus Christ as the sacrifice for
sin.

In order for man to enter the tabernacle, he had to
come through the gate. Even though the fence of righteousness kept the people away from the Lord, they could
gain access to Him if they came in His prescribed way.
This involved entering through the gate.

In this hanging, we have the Lord Jesus Christ as the
"way." There was no other entrance to the outer court, just
as there is no other way to God except through Jesus
Christ. Jesus said, "I am the door of the sheep. All that
ever came before me are thieves and robbers: but the
sheep did not hear them. I am the door: by me if any man
enter in, he shall be saved, and shall go in and out, and
find pasture" (John 10:7-9). Jesus additionally said, "I am
the way, . . . no man cometh unto the Father, but by me"
(John 14:6).

The gate of the tabernacle was wide enough to permit
access by any who desired to enter. But mark it well, the
moment that hanging was lifted up or pushed aside, it
brought whoever would enter there face to face with the
brazen altar, the altar of bloody sacrifice. One dare not
enter in without a sacrifice. He must himself bring the
sacrifice, slay it, shed its blood and appropriate it for himself. He had to confess it was the sole ground of his
approach to God.

We can approach the Father only through the Son. We
dare not approach God unless we come with full payment
for our sins. "Neither is there salvation in any other: for

there is none other name under heaven given among men, whereby we must be saved" (Acts 4:12). To reject Jesus Christ as Savior is to refuse to enter the only door to eternal life. We must come confessing our sins and accepting Jesus Christ as the substitute payment and sacrifice for our iniquities.

The wall, or fence, of fine white linen, represented God's perfect righteousness and said in effect, "Stay Out!" But the four-colored gate spoke of the mercy of God in Jesus Christ and said in effect, "Come In!"

## The Curtain at the Entrance of the Tabernacle

As one entered the tabernacle's outer court from the east, he first came to the brazen altar and then to the laver. Having made the proper sacrifice at the altar and having been cleansed at the laver, the priest was then prepared to enter the door into the Holy Place.

A curtain served as a door to the Holy Place. God instructed Moses: "And thou shalt make an hanging for the door of the tent, of blue, and purple, and scarlet, and fine twined linen, wrought with needlework" (Ex. 26:36).

From the dimensions of the tabernacle, we conclude this hanging was ten cubits wide by ten cubits high or fifteen by fifteen feet. The total area would be one hundred cubits, the same as the gate hanging and the vail. This hanging was held up by five pillars. These pillars were made of acacia wood and were overlaid with gold. They had gold caps and brass bases.

This door was likewise embroidered with colors of blue, purple and scarlet. As in all other places, the blue represents Heaven, the purple represents royalty and Heaven's payment for sin, the scarlet represents shed blood and sacrifice and the white material represents righteousness.

In harmony with the meaning of the word "hanging" this door served the purpose to keep some out and allow others to enter in. The fabric and colors are the same as the door to the courtyard and no doubt, equally represent Jesus Christ as the door. We have no clue as to what the design or the pattern of the colors were on the gate.

There is one clear difference between this door and the courtyard door. The requirements to enter this door are greater than merely entering the gate into the courtyard. After having offered certain sacrifices and then being cleansed at the laver, only certain priests could approach this door and enter in. The spiritual significance of this aspect of Christ's work must be found somewhere in the distinction between those that could enter through this hanging into the Holy Place. The idea is this: the closer we come to the Lord, the greater our relationship must be.

If the courtyard gate depicts Christ as the "way," then this door must depict Christ as the "truth." Furthermore, the vail is said to depict Christ as the "life." These entrances may very well represent Jesus Christ as the way, the truth and the life.

Not only was this entrance a door through which to pass, but upon entering it, there was a revelation of truth. Jesus said, "I am the way, the truth, and the life: no man cometh unto the Father, but by me" (John 14:6). In other words, to come unto the Father, one must come through the way, the truth and the life in the sense, that each of these is an entrance.

Although the hangings of the door shut off the Holy Place from the outer court, it formed an entrance for those who were qualified. Only certain priests who had made the proper sacrifices and been cleansed could make this closer approach to God. Jesus further taught that those who came to the truth could enjoy a closer and more intimate relationship to Him. He said: "If ye continue in my word, then are ye my disciples indeed (genuine); and ye shall know the truth, and the truth shall make you free" (John 8:31-32).

When the priest passed under the hanging he was face to face with the golden symbols within. In these symbols, he saw the truth of God's way in grace, in redemption and glory. Outside of that hanging, he could not know the truth of the tabernacle, the truth it alone could reveal. The greater the truth, the greater the knowledge one has of God Almighty, the greater the relationship will exist between the two.

Those who enter the Holy Place were allowed a closer approach and relationship to God. Salvation only is not enough. To know God as the bread of life, the light of the world, the intercessor, the King, the Savior is to be magnetically drawn to Him.

One door affords entrance into "life" and the other offers entrance into "life more abundantly" (John 10:10). Too many have entered only the first door and offered the sacrifices for sins for salvation. They need to enter also into a life filled with the truth and knowledge of God.

## The Vail

We now focus our attention on the vail that covered the entrance to the Holy of Holies. God gave the instructions for the making of the vail in Exodus 26:31-33. This hanging is given a special name called the "vail" in the Old Testament and spelled "veil" in the New Testament.

The vail was hung underneath the gold taches that connected the two sections of the linen curtains. The placement would have been twenty cubits from the front entrance which includes the front pillars of one cubit and eleven cubits from the rear wall. Behind the vail, and holding up the vail, were pillars of one cubit square, thus the distance from the back side of the pillars to the rear wall was exactly ten cubits. This gave the Holy of Holies an inside dimension of ten cubits cube.

The vail had the same dimensions as the entrance door to the tabernacle, being ten cubits wide by ten cubits high. Jewish tradition claims the thickness of the material in the Temple vail was a hand's breath, or about four inches thick.

The word "vail" is translated from a Hebrew word meaning "separation." With this thought added to the definition of "hanging," which means "to conceal, cover, protect, etc.," we have a double emphasis to the purpose of the vail. This word "vail" is a technical term not applied to any other curtain. The choice of this word implies a strong emphasis on "Do Not Enter!" Its connotation goes far beyond a mere separation of two rooms in the tabernacle, or Temple.

Like the other curtains, the vail was made of fine twined linen with embroidery of blue, purple and scarlet. The basic difference in the appearance is that cherubim were embroidered on the vail.

Parallel to the meaning of the other curtains and materials, the linen represents righteousness, blue signifies Heaven, purple pictures royalty and scarlet resembles blood sacrifice.

The cherubim were symbolic of protecting the holiness of God. They were placed on the east side of the Garden of Eden "to keep the way of the tree of life" (Gen. 3:24). Cherubim were embroidered into the linen covering over the tabernacle. They were also on the mercy seat where God communed with man (Ex. 25:22). On the vail entrance to the Holy of Holies, the cherubim represented the protection of the inner room where God's throne was. The presence of the cherubim was a warning: "Keep Out!"

To enter the courtyard, one must have salvation. To enter the Holy Place required a closer and more devoted life. But to enter the Holy of Holies, the very presence of God, required absolute perfection. The high priest was symbolic of the Lord Jesus Christ, and for that reason, he alone could enter the Most Holy Place. Until we are purged and cleansed, inside and out and completely made righteous, we can never enter into the very presence of God. For that reason, "no man hath seen God at any time."

If the courtyard gate pictures Christ as the "way," and the tabernacle entrance pictures Christ as the "truth," then the vail pictures Christ as the "life." We have a direct Scripture reference which states that the unrent vail was a symbol of the life, or humanity, of our Lord Jesus Christ.

"Having therefore, brethren, boldness to enter into the holiest by the blood of Jesus, by a new and living way, which he hath consecrated for us, through the veil, that is to say, his flesh" (Heb. 10:19-20). By "flesh" is meant, of course, our Lord's humanity.

The vail was the silent, but prophetic, declaration that God should be made manifest in the flesh; as it is written: "Without controversy great is the mystery of godliness: God was manifest in the flesh" (1 Tim. 3:16). "God was in Christ" (2 Cor. 5:19). "In him dwelleth all the fullness of the Godhead bodily" (Col. 2:9).

The vail is the perfect symbol and the absolute affirmation that "God was in Christ." So long as the vail hung down, it shut man out from the typical presence of God. So long as Christ walked the earth in His perfect humanity, He shut men out from God.

I. M. Halderman in his book *The Tabernacle, Priesthood and Offerings* has expressed this meaning as clearly as can be. He penned these words:

> If the humanity of Christ is the standard humanity in which alone God can enthrone Himself; if man must be as perfect as Christ was before God can take up His abode in him, before man can have fellowship and accepted and intimate relationship with God, then the Christ of God so far from being a way by which men can approach God, or God enter into man, becomes an impassable barrier, a terrific, concrete witness to the hopeless, and measureless distance between God and the natural man.

A man might stand before this vail as it hung down

between him and the symbolic dwelling place of God. He might admire the fineness of its texture, the perfectness of its coloring, the majesty and mystery of the winged figures; but the more he should look, the more he should study, the more evident it would become to him that in its imperviousness, even though beautiful, it shut him out from and entirely concealed the God who typically dwelt behind it.

We would see that all approach to the presence of God ended there. Let a man study intently and analytically the life of the Lord Jesus Christ. Let him take up His deeds, His words, His attitude to God and man, the more he studies, the more evident it will become that he and Jesus of Nazareth were not cast in the same mold, that they exist upon planes as far apart from each other as the east is from the west, as the ever receding west is from the east.

(Pages 127-128).

There was just one means by which that vail could be put aside as a barrier and become a way of entrance into the Holy of Holies. That one means was by the blood of the sacrifice victim shed on the brazen altar.

Once a year, on a day called "the day of atonement," the high priest went out to the brazen altar, took a bullock and a goat, slew them, put the blood in a basin, brought it into the Holy Place and sprinkled the blood before the vail. Having sprinkled the blood before the vail, he lifted up the vail, pushed it aside and entered the Most Holy Place. While there he sprinkled the blood upon the mercy seat. To have approached the Holy of Holies by any other means would have meant instant death.

Jesus revealed God's perfect holiness. As He walked on the earth, the Lord Jesus Christ revealed the standard man must attain if he expects to meet God. So Jesus revealed the impossibility of any approach to God unless the debt of sin could be paid and the person could become as holy as Christ.

People may admire the character and teachings of Christ in His earthly life, but the primary object of His life was to reveal God's holiness and to show that man is forever excluded from God unless he comes through Christ.

When Christ died, the vail of the Temple was rent in twain. The vail of the Temple was the same as that of the tabernacle in meaning and significance, but as to size it was larger being thirty feet high, thirty feet wide and four inches thick. The Bible gives special attention to the tearing of the vail at Christ's death. Luke records: "And it was about the sixth hour, and there was a darkness over all the earth until the ninth hour. And the sun was darkened, and the veil of the temple was rent in the midst" (Luke 23:44-45). Matthew states: "And, behold, the veil of the temple was rent in twain from the top to the bottom; and the earth did quake, and the rocks rent" (Matt. 27:51).

We must be made to realize that the death of Christ occurred on the annual day of Passover. This is not to be confused with the Day of Atonement. What Christ symbolically did on the Day of Atonement was literally carried out on the Jewish day of Passover. The day of Passover occurred annually on the 14th of Nisan.

It is appropriate that the death of Christ would take place on this day. For over 1,400 years the Jews faithfully observed the Passover. Over 1,400 times the Jews had symbolically crucified Christ. Each time, a paschal lamb was sacrificed which represented the offering of Jesus Christ.

It was sacrificed at the altar which represents the cross of Calvary. Paul said: "For even Christ our passover is sacrificed for us" (1 Cor. 5:7b). John the Baptist identified Christ by saying: "Behold the Lamb of God, which taketh away the sin of the world" (John 1:29).

It was on the 14th day of Nisan, the day of Passover, that Jesus and His disciples made preparation for the Passover. By the time of Christ, minor changes had been made in the observance of the Passover. Instead of each family killing the animal at home, it was brought to the tabernacle or Temple and slain there. Certain parts were burned on the altar, the blood was poured out at the base of the altar, and the flesh was taken to the home and roasted. Sometimes several small families, or friends would prepare the lamb and eat the Passover supper together. Such was the case of Jesus and His disciples eating together. According to Mark 14:12, the disciples had taken the lamb to the altar and slew it and made the other preparations for them to eat the supper together.

All this took place early in the Jewish day. The lamb was slain between sundown and darkness. It was then roasted and the rest of the meal prepared. By the time they ate the meal it would have been around nine or ten o'clock in the evening at the earliest. After finishing the Passover feast, Jesus took the ingredients of unleavened bread and wine and instituted the ordinance of the Lord's Supper in His church. By virtue of this ordinance, He wants us never to forget the sacrifice of Himself, the breaking of His body and the spilling of His blood. The Passover supper persistently declared that there would be a sacrificial substitute for man's sin. The Lord's Supper is a ceaseless reminder that the Lord has shed His blood and broken His body for our sins. It is only when we realize this, that we can observe the Lord's Supper with true spiritual meaning.

From the supper table, Jesus and His disciples went into the garden to pray. It was there the traitor Judas betrayed Jesus with a kiss, and He was taken captive by the servants of the high priest. It was here with the betrayal kiss that the God of Heaven turned His back upon His Son, and Jesus was left to do His work alone.

He was led away in the wee hours of the morning, probably around two or three o'clock in the morning, to the series of mock trials. With the aid of lying witnesses,

Jesus was declared guilty of sin worthy of death. By the demands of an angry mob shouting "Crucify him! Crucify him!" Pilate led Him away to be crucified.

It was about the third hour (nine o'clock in the morning), while the Roman soldiers were driving the nails into the hands and feet of Jesus, the priests were busy in the courtyard of the Temple offering the daily sacrifice. These offerings were called "whole burnt-offerings," because the entire animal was consumed upon the altar, and further because they symbolized the Lord Jesus Christ in giving His all upon the altar. The Bible declares "ye are bought with a price." For all else, God could just speak and create anything He wanted. He wanted a universe; and He just spoke and there it was. But for our sins, the price had to be paid. God could not create the payment; He had to pay it Himself. It is the only thing God ever had to buy. Imagine, God having to pay for something! The price was tremendous. It was so great that it cost God everything an almighty God could afford. It cost God His only begotten Son. Not one red cent could be added to the price that God paid for our sins. It was the greatest price paid for anything, ever!

Jesus hung there on the cross for six painful and agonizing hours. From the third hour to the ninth hour, from nine o'clock in the morning to three o'clock in the afternoon. At the sixth hour darkness was upon the earth until the ninth hour. At the ninth hour Jesus uttered: "My God, my God, why hast thou forsaken me?" Following these words, He spoke His last from the cross: "Father, into thy hands I commend my spirit" (Luke 23:46). And He died.

The ninth hour, or three o'clock in the afternoon, was the time of the evening sacrifice. It too was a whole burnt-offering. While the lamb was being slain outside in the courtyard, two priests were in the Holy Place. One was trimming the lamp stand, and the other was offering incense on the altar of incense, which was immediately in front of the vail.

It was the ninth hour at three o'clock in the afternoon, the time of the evening sacrifice, that Jesus died and gave up the Ghost. In the courtyard as the priest was drawn back to slay the animal, Jesus died. The priest was symbolically doing in the courtyard what Jesus was literally doing on the cross. At the exact same time, in the Holy Place, another priest was offering incense on the altar of incense. The altar of incense was located in the middle of the room next to the veil. Hence, the priest was standing immediately in front of the veil "And, behold, the veil of the temple was rent in twain from the top to the bottom; and the earth did quake, and the rocks rent." That vail, thirty feet wide and thirty feet wide and four inches thick, ripped from the top to the bottom. The sound of that rip was deafening. That priest saw something he had never seen in his life - the inside of the Holy of Holies. What a frightful experience! For the first time in his life, he gazed into the Holy of Holies.

The vail is rent! The way is open! And we now have free access into the very presence of God through the rent body of Jesus Christ. The rending of that beautiful vail symbolized the rending of the wondrous life of the Lord Jesus and the payment in full for our sins. When the vail was rent, it changed at once from a barrier to an open way to the throne of God. We may now come to the throne of grace. We may come freely whenever we care, as often as we please, and stay as long as we wish. We can approach God as righteous, not by our own righteousness, but by the imputed righteousness of Christ.

In the tabernacle and the Temple, the Holy Place with the altar of incense was separated from the Holy of Holies by means of the vail. In John's vision of Heaven, he saw the throne of God and the altar of incense next to it with no barrier (Rev. 8:3). For all practical purposes, these items were intended to be together at the throne of God. But perfect righteousness, as exhibited by the life of Christ, prevented our being able to come directly to the presence of God with our prayers. But through the rent body of Jesus, our sins are paid and the righteousness of Christ is imputed to us, and we have free access to the very throne of God in Heaven. We pray to the Father, "in Jesus' name" or literally "by His authority." Through Jesus Christ we are given the authority and privilege of going directly to the throne of the Father in Heaven.

The vail was rent from the top to the bottom, not from the bottom to the top. It was a miracle. No human hand could have done the work of rending the vail. The vail in the temple at the time of Christ was so woven together that rabbinical writers claim that two pairs of oxen (that's four on each side) attached to either edge and driven in opposite directions could not tear it asunder. It hung in a loose fold and could not be cut or torn by a direct stroke; it was too soft and yielding for that. Neither was it so fixed that an earthquake could affect it. The rending of the vail was an act of God!

Tradition also claims that the priests tried to mend and sew the vail together again but were unable to, for no thread, no cord, would hold in the repaired part. It was rent once for all and forever. What a picture; God rent the life of His perfect Son to make the payment for the sins of mankind so that the way would be open and they would have access to the presence of God.

We must clearly understand that the death of Christ was also the act of God and not man. When the band of Temple guards came to Gethsemane to take Jesus prisoner, Jesus asked them: "Whom seek ye?" One of them replies: "Jesus of Nazareth." As Jesus responded, "I am he," we are told "they went backward, and fell to the ground." A man in his right mind should have gotten up, dusted himself off, and went home. They could only approach Jesus with His permission, much less take Him prisoner.

Simon Peter realizing what was about to happen, having a sword, drew it and smote the high priest's servant named Malchus and cut off his right ear. Jesus stops Peter, and then tenderly walks up to the servant and heals him on the spot. In the presence of this mob, Jesus works another miracle showing positive proof that He is the Messiah.

Jesus then turns His attention to Peter. He tells him to put up the sword. As he does, Jesus said to Peter: "Thinkest thou that I cannot now pray to my Father, and he shall presently give me more than twelve legions of angels?" Think of it! More than 72,000 angels, in the heavens just above their heads, unseen to the eyes of men, ready and prepared to come to the defense of Jesus. If one angel, in one night, killed 185,000 soldiers of the army of Sennacherib, just imagine the mincemeat 72,000 angels could have done to the world at the command of Jesus! There they were, in the darkness, 72,000 angry, militant angels just waiting for the Lord to give the command: "Come on boys!" And some people have the bright idea that the soldiers "took" Jesus by force. Jesus was taken prisoner because He wanted to be.

Before the judges and authorities, Jesus did not even give them the dignity of answering their charges. After all, He wasn't there because He had to be; He was there because that's where He chose to be at the time. I used to wonder as a young Christian why Jesus did not defend Himself, until I realized that they were doing what they were, only because Jesus gave them permission to do it. This scenario was planned in Heaven before the foundation of the world. It was an appointment in the fullness of time that God made with man.

Pilate became a little frustrated because of Jesus' silence and told Jesus: "Knowest thou not that I have power to crucify thee, and have power to release thee?" That statement got a response from Jesus. Jesus looked at Pilate with eye-piercing contact, and as sternly as He had said anything replied: "Thou couldest have no power at all against me, except it were given thee from above.'

The Scriptures declare He "gave himself for us." Jesus told His disciples: "I lay down my life, that I might take it again. No man taketh it from me, but I lay it down of myself. I have power to lay it down, and I have power to take it again" (John 10:17-18). You cannot charge the Jews with the murder of Jesus. You can only charge them with the intent to commit murder.

In Matthew's record, it is said that Christ "yielded" up the ghost. This word yield means "to send away for forth." Jesus did not die from the crucifixion or the beatings. He died when He ordered His spirit to leave Him. Man did not kill Jesus. He gave Himself for us. He died voluntary of His own choice that we might live.

Hallelujah! What a Savior!

# CHAPTER SEVEN

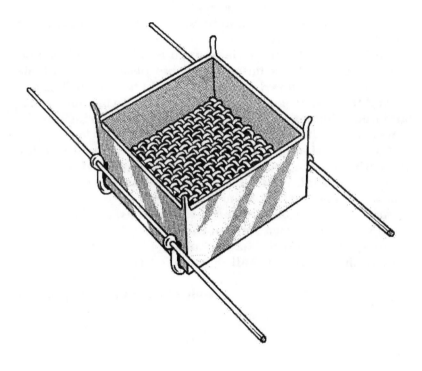

# THE ALTAR OF
# SACRIFICE

And thou shalt make an altar [of] shittim wood, five cubits long, and five cubits broad; the altar shall be foursquare: and the height thereof [shall be] three cubits.

And thou shalt make the horns of it upon the four corners thereof: his horns shall be of the same: and thou shalt overlay it with brass.

And thou shalt make his pans to receive his ashes, and his shovels, and his basons, and his fleshhooks, and his firepans: all the vessels thereof thou shalt make [of] brass.

And thou shalt make for it a grate of network [of] brass; and upon the net shalt thou make four brasen rings in the four corners thereof.

And thou shalt put it under the compass of the altar beneath, that the net may be even to the midst of the altar.

And thou shalt make staves for the altar, staves [of] shittim wood, and overlay them with brass.

And the staves shall be put into the rings, and the staves shall be upon the two sides of the altar, to bear it.

Hollow with boards shalt thou make it: as it was shewed thee in the mount, so shall they make [it].

**Exodus 27:1-8; Cf. Exodus 38:1-7**

# THE BRAZEN ALTAR OF SACRIFICE

There were exactly seven articles of furniture in the tabernacle, every piece of which is charged with meaning and stands to declare the plans and purposes of God. In the outer court of the tabernacle were two pieces of furniture: the brazen altar and the brazen layer. In the Holy Place there were three pieces of furniture: the golden candlestick, the table of shewbread and the altar of incense. Inside the Holy of Holies were two pieces of furniture that had the appearance of one: the ark of the covenant and the mercy seat.

Seven is the number of perfection. The seven pieces of furniture tell us of God's perfect provision for us to fellowship and associate with Him.

## Building An Altar

The brazen altar was the first piece of furniture the sinner encountered as he passed through the gate on his way to fellowship with and worship God. The details of its construction are found in Exodus 27:1-8. Unless he settled the matter of the judgment of his sins at the altar, he could proceed no further. Unless one stops at the altar, accepts the sacrifice and appropriates the blood, there is no further progress.

The altar was in the form of a hollow box: seven and one-half feet (five cubits) square; and four and one-half feet (three cubits) high. It was without a base or a top and was thus hollow inside. There were four brass horns made into each corner. As to the matter of the "grate of network" and the "compass," the language is not clear enough to give us an exact description.

The compass of the altar was a small ledge running around the inside of the altar exactly halfway between the top and the bottom. Additionally, there was a "grate of network of brass" that was to go under the inside ledge. It apparently rested up against the ledge as the grate of brass was to sit at the same place as the compass "even to the midst of the altar." Attached to the grate of brass were four rings with which the altar was transported. Exactly how these rings were attached to the network of brass is not known. We would normally think that the brass grating would lay on top of the ledge for support, but that is not the case. The inside ledge of the altar rested on the brass grating. It simply appears that the entire altar consisted of two pieces: the main body and the grating.

It is apparent that the fire was built under this network of brass, and the animal, when sacrificed, would be laid upon this network of brass. The fire would come up through the grating of brass and consume the animal. There was a continual operation without interruption. The offerings were continually added to the altar from the top, while the wood was being added underneath. Yet the ashes could constantly be removed. Jewish tradition asserts that the ashes were cleaned out very early each morning. They were taken to a clean place outside the camp and disposed.

## Rated Fireproof

The question has continually been raised whether the altar, built of wood and overlaid in brass, would be able to withstand the heat generated by the fire needed to consume so many sacrifices. The claim has been made that in recent years a discovery was made by scientists that wood overlaid with brass, the joints of which were hermetically (vacuum) sealed, was rated "fireproof" which could withstand 1500 degrees for one hour. This was considered a modern invention, but it certainly answers the query of the brazen altar and stands as a witness to the accuracy of the Bible. We have to admit, God is a pretty good scientist. It took man 3,500 years to figure out it would work.

## The Accessories

In addition to the altar, there were five accessories or utensils mentioned. "And thou shalt make his pans to receive his ashes, and his shovels, and his basons, and his fleshhooks, and his firepans: all the vessels thereof thou shalt make of brass" (Ex. 27:3). The pans were used to carry the ashes from the altar to a special place outside the camp. The shovels were used for picking up the ashes and for feeding the fire. The basins held the blood of the victims which usually was poured out at the base of the altar, but sometimes carried inside the tabernacle. The fleshhooks adjusted the pieces of the sacrificial animal upon the altar. We are told they were a three-pronged instrument (1 Sam. 2:13). And last, the firepans, sometimes called "censers," carried the burning embers from the brazen altar to the altar of incense. In all probability, this is why they are called censers. All of these utensils were made of brass.

Along with the already mentioned accessories, there were specially prepared coverings used to cover the altar when it was being transported. These coverings are mentioned in Numbers 4:13-14: "And they shall take away the ashes from the altar, and spread a purple cloth thereon: and they shall put upon it all the vessels thereof, wherewith they minister about it, even the censers, the fleshhooks, and the shovels, and the basons, all the vessels of the altar; and they shall spread upon it a covering of badgers' skins, and put to the staves of it."

## Moving the Altar

The coverings consisted of two items: the cloth, made of linen dyed purple, and the badgers' skins. No dimension is given for these coverings and their only requirement was to cover the altar and accessories. The covering of badgers' skins has been dealt with under the topic of the coverings of the tabernacle. Of all the furniture, the brazen altar is the only item to be covered with a cloth of purple when being transported. Purple is the combination of blue, the color of Heaven, and scarlet, the color of the sin payment of blood. This is a fitting color for this covering. As the altar represents the cross, it was at the cross that the Son of God from Heaven shed His blood as payment for sin.

The question is often raised that since the altar was to be kept burning continually, was it still burning during transport? The answer is obviously no. When being transported, the tabernacle was not in operation. The cloud was removed and the operations of the tabernacle were temporarily halted. Besides, the ashes were removed from the altar, and it was covered with a purple cloth and badgers' skins. This would not allow for a fire to be burning. It is likely a censer may have been filled with live coals and then used to reignite the fire of the altar.

Originally, the brass outer walls of the brazen altar were smooth and polished. For years they remained unchanged until the rebellion of Korah and his followers brought the judgment of God down on them. These rebellious people had come before the Lord sacrilegiously with brazen incense censers. Struck dead by the fire of God, they let their censers fall to the ground. At the command of the Lord, these censers were gathered and hammered each one into a flat plate. These plates were either attached to the sides of the brazen altar in plain view or were made as a detachable covering (Num. 16:36-40). It was an all-time warning that one not qualified should not strive for the office and ministry of priest.

The altar was located in a strategic location. This was the first article of furniture the sinner passing through the eastern gate encountered. It stood between the gate of the court and the approach to the tabernacle. There was no approach to the tabernacle except by way of this altar. Until one stops at the altar, accepts the sacrifice and appropriates the blood, there is no further progress. It was both a way to God and a barrier to God. If the Israelite brought his offering to the priest, and it was offered on the altar, then he could freely approach into the presence of the Lord. If a man endeavored to approach without a substitute, it meant certain death. The altar was a barrier to any man who sought to draw near to the tabernacle that did not own and confess an atoning sacrifice for himself on the altar. The consuming fire of the altar spoke of the judgment of God against him and shut him out of the congregation of God.

## The Spiritual Significance

This is the very heart of the spiritual significance of the altar. The offering on the altar was actually a type of Christ who became the substitute for man's sin and thus allowed the holy God and sinful man to meet. The altar was the place of substitutionary sacrifices, the place of death. There the body was consumed by fire, and the blood was poured out signifying that the judgment of God was satisfied. The word translated "altar" is from a Hebrew word meaning "slaughter place."

The altar is a type of the cross of Calvary. It was there that Jesus sacrificed Himself and shed His blood for the sin of the world. These daily sacrifices offered on the altar pointed to Jesus Christ who was sacrificed on the cross. Concerning His sacrifice Hebrews 9:25-28 says:

> Nor yet that he should offer himself often, as the high priest entereth into the holy place every year with blood of others;
> For then must he often have suffered since the foundation of the world: but now once in the end of

the world hath he appeared to put away sin by the sacrifice of himself.

And as it is appointed unto men once to die, but after this the judgment:

So Christ was once offered to bear the sins of many; and unto them that look for him shall he appear the second time without sin unto salvation.

Christ's one offering on the cross literally put away the sins that were pictorially covered by the tabernacle offerings on the altar. The offerings on the altar only symbolized the true substitutionary sacrifice, Jesus Christ. Hebrews 10:1 says, "For the law having a shadow of good things to come, and not the very image of the things, can never with those sacrifices which they offered year by year continually make the comers thereunto perfect." Verse 4 states, "For it is not possible that the blood of bulls and of goats should take away sins." Christ's one sacrifice forever is spoken of in verse 12: But this man, after he had offered one sacrifice for sins for ever, sat down on the right hand of God."

The offerer brought his offering personally and willingly. The sinner coming to the brazen altar was to put his hands upon the head of the animal, thus identifying the offering as his. In doing so, he was confessing his sins and his need of a substitute to suffer his punishment in his stead. The offerer must then slay the animal himself, being totally responsible for the death of the animal.

We, too, must come to Christ personally and willingly. We must confess to Him our sins and our need of Him being our substitute for our punishment. We must realize that we personally are responsible for the death of Christ on the cross. Upon the confession of our sins and the acceptance of Jesus Christ as our substitute, we can enter into the presence and fellowship of God.

At the top of the altar were four horns, one on each corner. Horns in the Scriptures are symbolic of power and strength. The psalmist speaks of binding the sacrifice to the horns of the altar (Psalm 118:27). Instances occur in Scripture of those who sought refuge by taking hold of the horns of the altar.  There was  Adonijah who "feared because of Solomon. and arose, and went, and caught hold on the horns of the altar" (1 Kings 1:50). There was Joab, who "fled unto the tabernacle of the LORD, and caught hold on the horns of the altar" (1 Kings 2:28-29). As symbols of power and authority, they pointed to the four corners of the earth, indicating through the sacrifice of Calvary, that salvation is available to all men: "for the sins of the whole world" (1 John 2:2).

The altar had two staves by which it was carried from place to place. These staves passed through four brass rings attached to the sides of the altar. These staves were made of wood and overlaid in brass. The altar was not to be carried about on a wagon, but was to be borne upon the shoulders of the priests.

Right after the first sacrifice was laid on the altar, "there came a fire out from before the LORD, and consumed upon the altar the burnt-offering and the fat: which when all the people saw, they shouted, and fell on their faces" (Lev. 9:24). God showed His acceptance of the sacrifice by sending the first fire and saying, "The fire shall ever be burning upon the altar; it shall never go out" (Lev. 6:13). Why never go out? Because the people would never stop sinning, and the sacrifice was made only as a continual symbol of the sacrifice of Christ. Fire has always symbolized God's judgment. We should be glad that the fire fell on the sacrifice on the altar to show that God accepted it and that judgment need not fall on us.

## Common Procedures for Sacrifices

For all the animal sacrifices held at the altar, there were certain common procedures. The offerer would bring the animal that personally belonged to him. He would be met just outside the entrance by a priest. The priest would ask the nature of the sacrifice and then examine the animal for qualifications. The animal had to be the right animal for the sacrifice and had to be without spot or blemish. After all, Jesus was perfect and the animal had to represent the perfect Christ. He would then be admitted into the courtyard, after taking off his shoes and leaving them on the outside.

Once inside the courtyard, the offerer would proceed to the right, to the north side of the altar. There he would be assisted by another priest. His animal would be confined by some means so as to prevent its escape. The offerer would then lay both hands on the head of the animal. For all intent and purposes, he was to offer a prayer stating that he had sinned worthy of death and that his guilt was being transferred to the animal and the innocent animal was going to die in his place.

The priest would direct the offerer to place one hand on the neck of the animal. He showed him were the jugular vein was located and how to take his fingers and squeeze the vein. The priest would hand him a very sharp knife, and the offerer would place it beside his hand and give a quick cut to the neck of the animal. It was the most humane means of slaying the animal. The heart would pump the blood out and the animal would quietly and painlessly die. The priest did not kill the animal for the offerer. The sinner was personally responsible for the death of the animal.

With the throat cut, the priest quickly steps in with a brass basin to collect the blood. The blood is considered holy and only the priest can handle it. Most commonly, the blood was poured out on or about the brazen altar.

The flesh of the animal was handled in different ways. Sometimes the animal was slain and burned on the altar itself. Often the animal was slain and then carried to a clean place outside the camp and burned. On occasions, the animal was eaten by the priests in the courtyard. And finally, sometimes the animal was slain at the altar and carried back to the home of the offerer and eaten there.

The offering on the altar was actually a type of Christ who became the substitute for man's sin and who died as the true sacrifice for our sins. The brazen altar was a type of the cross of Calvary. It was there that Jesus sacrificed Himself and shed His blood for the sin of the world.

## The Five Levitical Offerings

There were five Levitical offerings listed in the first six chapters of the book of Leviticus. All offerings fit into these five categories. The Leviticus list occurs in a sequence of popularity, that is, beginning with the highest number of offerings to the smallest. The actual order that one might offer the sacrifices might differ from the order of the list.

People are inclined to think that one would be going to the altar every other day having to make a sacrifice. It is true that we sin a lot, but it was not required that we make a sacrifice that often. When the sacrifices were made, they were made with emotion and enthusiasm. The offerer understanding the significance of the sacrifice did not offer it in a cold, meaningless ceremony.

### Sin Offering:

The first sacrifice one offered in his lifetime would have been the sin offering. The sin offering was for sins of ignorance. This offering covered our inherent sin nature. It pictured our salvation. The offering itself did not bring salvation to the sinner, but rather was offered representing that the sinner had already been saved. We not only need to be saved from the things we have done, but need to be saved from what we are, a sinner.

Depending on the position and rank in life of the person making this offering, the sacrifice was handled differently. For the common person, the animal was eaten by the priests. In the event, the person was a ruler or leader, the animal was taken outside the camp and burned in a clean place. The idea is that with rank comes responsibility, and that the sins of leaders are greater than that of the common people.

## Trespass Offering:

The second offering that might be offered was a trespass offering. Even after we have been saved, and our soul cleansed and sealed, we continue to sin in the flesh. It is God's will that we grow in spiritual maturity and overcome the sins of the flesh. But, sometimes we let our flesh nature get out of control and we may backslide. The trespass offering was for the backslider who had repented and returned to the Lord.

Some people are saved and make a commitment of service to the Lord and never waver in their lifetime. Now there are those times when we are spiritually colder than other times, but that does not mean we have backslidden. A backslider is one who has gotten away from the Lord and has abandoned his prayer life, his Bible study, his worship attendance and his testimony. When he awakens from his spiritual condition and once again seeks the Lord, he would offer a trespass offering as a public testimony that he has returned to the Lord. Some saved people would never have to make this sacrifice. The animals required and the manner of making this sacrifice were the same as the sin offering.

## The Whole Burnt Offering

Once a person was saved, and once a person rededicated his life, then he could offer a burnt offering. The burnt offering was most commonly a lamb. The animal was brought to the altar and slain. It was cut up into pieces without breaking any bones. The whole animal was burned on the altar.

Pertaining to Christ, the whole burnt offering represented His total surrender to be a sacrifice for our sins. The animal had to belong to the person making the offering. It was an extension of the offerer. It was the representative of the offerer. The person who made this offering was in effect surrendering his whole being to the Lord. It is like a person today coming to the altar and making it known to his family, friends and church that he wants to live completely for the Lord.

The whole burnt offering could be offered alone, but it always accompanied a sin offering and a trespass offering. It assumed that a person just saved, or one who had just rededicated his life also intended to dedicate his heart, soul and life to the service of the Lord.

One might offer this sacrifice once with the sin offering, make a commitment to God, and need not to have to offer it again.

**The Peace Offering:**

The peace offering was the most joyous of all the sacrifices. It was rendered out of a heart filled with the joy of the Lord. It was literally a "thanksgiving" offering. It was offered in the proper sequence. First, one has to be saved. Secondly, one has to confess all his sins. Thirdly, he dedicates his life to God. Then, he has peace with God. One would offer this offering any time his heart overflowed with the goodness of God. It might be that God has blessed him with a bountiful harvest. It might be that the Lord answered a very important prayer. He would offer this sacrifice to God out of a heart filled with generosity.

Most commonly this sacrifice was reserved for special occasions. The head of the household may offer it in behalf of the whole family. It would commonly be done at family reunions. The head of the house would take the animal to the altar and slay it there. Certain portions went to the officiating priest, but the rest of the animal was kept by the offerer. He would return to his home with the animal and then roast it. With all the family, friends, and the neighborhood Levites and priests assembled, they would eat the peace offering with great celebration.

In the case of the peace offering we learn that we have peace with God through the sacrifice of Jesus Christ. With the family and friends together we learn that when we have peace with God, we have peace with each other.

Is not this the same order of service today? First, we are saved. Secondly, we confess our daily sins. Third, we surrender our hearts and lives to the Lord. Then, after that, we have peace with God. The order of the Old Testament sacrifices is the same as our order of service to God today.

## The Meat Offering:

What is strange is that with all the animal sacrifices we come to the meat offering that did not have any meat in it. This term was borrowed from the British. When the British speak of eating, they speak of meat. The meat offering was literally a food offering. It was offered in one of three forms. It could be roasted grain, or ground flour, or baked cakes.

The word for meat offering comes from a word meaning "gift" or "present." One would bring this offering whenever he offered the burnt offerings. It would be brought to the altar, and a small portion would be pinched off and placed on the altar. The rest of the offering would go to the priests. It was part of their pay for rendering service in the sanctuary of the Lord.

In bringing this offering to the altar, the offerer was bringing a gift to God. God had done so much for him, now he brings a present to God as a token of his recognition of what God has done for him. It is true, that if we are saved, we ought to be giving something back to God for all He has done for us.

# CHAPTER EIGHT

# WASHING AT
# THE LAVER

And the LORD spake unto Moses, saying,

Thou shalt also make a laver [of] brass, and his foot [also of] brass, to wash [withal]: and thou shalt put it between the tabernacle of the congregation and the altar, and thou shalt put water therein.

For Aaron and his sons shall wash their hands and their feet thereat:

When they go into the tabernacle of the congregation, they shall wash with water, that they die not; or when they come near to the altar to minister, to burn offering made by fire unto the LORD:

So they shall wash their hands and their feet, that they die not: and it shall be a statute for ever to them, [even] to him and to his seed throughout their generations. .

**Exodus 30:17-21**

# WASHING AT THE LAVER

The second piece of furniture found in the outer court was the brazen laver. It stood between the brazen altar where they sacrificed the animals and the tabernacle building.

One had to settle the matter of sin at the brazen altar before he approached the laver. Hence, the person who approached the laver would already be saved. Before a priest could enter the tabernacle proper, he had to wash his hands and feet at the laver "that they die not" (Ex. 30:17-21).

Additional information is found in two other passages of Scripture regarding the laver. Exodus 38:8, "And he made the laver of brass and the foot of it of brass, of the lookingglasses of the women assembling, which assembled at the door of the tabernacle of the congregation." Exodus 40:7 reads: "And thou shalt set the laver between the tent of the congregation and the altar, and shalt put water therein."

Laver is the same word from which we get our word "lavatory." The Hebrew word means to "make round, hence pot, basin." We know nothing about the size or shape of the laver for no dimensions or directions are given for making it. The very meaning of the word indicates that it was a round basin, and this view is universally accepted.

Another omission regarding it is that it was not specially committed to any of the Levite families, and there was no provision made for carrying it through the wilderness. However, we understand the Kohathites would naturally have been in charge as they were with all the other pieces of furniture. When the coverings are mentioned with respect to the transporting the furniture, all mention of the laver is omitted. It is only mentioned once after the account of its construction and placing when Moses anointed it (Lev. 8:11). The laver is never mentioned again, and Solomon's "sea" is the first we hear of anything taking its place.

The laver was made from the brass "looking glasses (polished brass mirrors) of the women ... which assembled at the door of the tabernacle" (Ex. 38:8). These women, assembled at the door of the tabernacle, were probably the women who were busy making the curtains and doing the embroidery work and other possible tasks. In our version, the word "women" is in italics because the word is not found in the original text. It is translated appropriately because the word "assembling" is in the feminine gender.

Each time the laver is mentioned, the "foot' is mentioned separately: "laver, and his foot." Because of this and the fact that little detailed information is given on the construction of the laver, much "speculative theology" has been advanced on the topic. The word "foot" is not the most popular translation from the original Hebrew word. Scholars claim the Hebrew word means "base" or "pedestal." The most popular position is that the foot to the laver was a base or pedestal on which it sat, making the whole thing a two piece construction.

However, not all agree that the foot was a pedestal. There are several who argue that it was a reservoir and that together the laver and foot had the appearance of a cup and saucer. The question keeps coming to mind, if the foot was a basin like the laver or even a base with a built-in bowl, why was an appropriate word not used? The word "foot" clearly means a base or pedestal, and it is a stretch of the imagination to make it another bowl. It is the opinion of this author that the foot was nothing more than a base on which the laver sat, but it is only fair to the reader to mention that other positions exist.

After all, they would never contaminate the entire basin of water by actually placing their bloody hands and dirty feet into the laver. After the first priest stuck his bloody hands and dirty feet into the laver, who would want to wash his hands in that water?

Jewish tradition claims that the laver was a reservoir with spouts or cocks from which the water was poured and the priests would wash. At the least, there were probably dippers used to dip the water from the laver and from which the priests would wash. The text does not say that the priests were to wash themselves IN the basin, but AT it. The priest did not wash IN the laver because the water in which they washed would then have been rendered impure by those who washed before or with them. It was not the Jewish custom at any time to wash in a basin but at a falling stream where each successive cleansing was of clean water. Furthermore, certain parts of the sacrifices had to be washed before being placed on the altar. Again, the water was probably taken from the laver and poured over the flesh.

Since there is an omission of details regarding the means of transporting, no mention of coverings during a move and no information on utensils such as buckets, dippers and so forth, it is concluded that the probability of spouts or basins is there but lost in the lack of information. Such apparatus probably existed separate from the laver and its foot.

The brazen laver stood in the courtyard between the altar and the tabernacle. One could not be cleansed at the laver unless the sacrifice was first made at the altar. And one could not approach and enter the tabernacle unless he had first been cleansed at the laver.

The purpose of the laver is stated in Exodus 30:19-21:

For Aaron and his Sons shall wash their hands and their feet thereat:
When they go into the tabernacle of the congrega-

tion, they shall wash with water, that they die not; or
when they come near to the altar to minister, to burn
offering made by fire unto the LORD:
So they shall wash their hands and their feet, that
they die not.

Notice the purpose of the laver as the priests were to
wash both their hands and their feet at the laver before
proceeding into the Holy Place. The floor of the tabernacle was simply the dust of the desert, so the priests' feet
would need daily washing. Having offered sacrifices, the
priests' hands would need to be washed. If a priest
endeavored to enter the tabernacle before his hands and
his feet were cleansed, he would die. The laver was provided so that he would not be struck dead by God.

As to the symbolical significance of the laver, most
writers are in harmony. The laver was made of solid brass
and was filled with pure water. Brass in the Scripture
speaks of the judgment of God, able to withstand the fire
of testing. Water is symbolic of the Word of God. Here at
the laver the sins of the saints are taken care of. At the
brazen altar, the penalty of sin was settled forever, but at
the laver, the defilement of sins committed by the believer after regeneration is provided for completely. The laver
speaks of separation from the world through confession of
sin and cleansing by the Word of God. It speaks of self-
judgment and a yielding to God for His service alone.

The laver and the water in it are both symbolical of the
Word of God and the cleansing or sanctification that
comes through the Word of God. The Scriptures frequently speak of the cleansing that comes through the application of the Word.

The laver was made of the "lookingglasses" of the
women. These were highly polished brass mirrors. The
fact that the Word of God is a "lookingglass" is so indicated in James 1: 23-25:

For if any be a hearer of the word, and not a doer, he is like unto a man beholding his natural face in a glass:

For he beholdeth himself, and goeth his way, and straightway forgetteth what manner of man he was.

But whoso looketh into the perfect law of liberty, and continueth therein, he being not a forgetful hearer, but a doer of the work, this man shall be blessed in his deed.

## Be Sure To Wash Your Hands And Feet

Every time a priest would enter the tabernacle he would first have to stop at the laver and wash his hands and feet "that they die not." A priest might wash his hands and feet many more times at the laver than just those times he would go into the tabernacle. Every time he completed killing, butchering and burning the animal, he would come to the laver and wash. He washed dozens of times per day at the laver. He might not even enter the tabernacle while working in the courtyard, but he would often wash at the laver.

For certain, each time a priest entered into the tabernacle, whether he had just finished a sacrifice or not, he had to stop first and wash his hands and feet at the laver. The priest who would serve in the tabernacle must daily wash his hands and feet at the laver. Hands are for service, and feet are for walk. The Christian who would serve the Lord effectively, must also walk before the Lord acceptably.

## The Laver Does Not Represent Baptism.

Many students of the tabernacle will associate washing at the laver and then entering into the tabernacle a type of baptism which is necessary before entering into membership in a church. This takes us back to a point

already made that there are many similarities between
Old Testament worship and New Testament worship.
But because two things are similar does not make one
necessarily symbolical of the other. If baptism is symbolized by washing at the laver, then baptism is pictured as
an act by pouring or sprinkling. Do you think that if a
young boy asked a priest the significance of his washing
at the laver that the priest would respond by saying,
"Son, washing at the laver symbolizes being baptized so
one could enter a church." And then imagine the son asking, "Priest, what is a church?" and the priest respond-
ing, "Son, I don't have a clue. A church is a mystery to
us." I cannot conceive that the significance of the washing at the laver was going to represent something that
could not be understood by the Jewish worshipper.

## What Does The Washing Mean?

What is the significance of washing at the laver? The
laver is going to speak of the daily and regular cleansing
of our outward lives as Christians. At the brazen sacrificial altar, the penalty of sin was settled forever, but at
the brazen laver the defilement of sins committed by the
believer after regeneration is provided for completely.
The laver speaks of the continual sanctification of our
lives.

The priests' feet would be defiled from the dust of the
ground and their hands from the handling of the bloody
sacrifices. This required a continual cleansing at the
laver. Our sins are atoned for at the sacrificial altar and
we are saved there. Our soul is saved and sealed, but our
outward nature continues to sin. We need a continual
cleansing or sanctification of the flesh nature to bring it
under control. The cleansing at the laver is typical of the
continual cleansing and sanctification of the flesh
nature.

## Washing By Water Represents The Cleansing That Comes Through Regular Bible Study

Water and cleansing by water is symbolical of the cleansing that comes to us through regular Bible study. John 17:17 says, "Sanctify them through thy truth: thy word is truth." Sanctify means to wash or cleanse. Question: how are we cleansed? Answer: through truth, that is, the Word of God.

Psalm 119:9, asks a question: "Wherewith shall a young man cleanse his way? by taking heed thereto according to thy Word." A young man cleanses himself through the Word of God. Speaking of the church, it is said, "That he might sanctify and cleanse it with the washing of water by the word" (Eph. 5:26). The Word of God has a cleansing effect upon the members of a church. And one last reference: "Now ye are clean through the word which I have spoken to you" (John 15:3). These verses are sufficient to show that the study of the Bible has a cleansing effect upon our old, fleshly, sinful nature.

While we are justified in Christ and saved, we are still in the world of defilement and of sin. We are constantly exposed to and subjected to sin in our business, social, personal and even religious lives. There is a constant need for cleansing. That continual cleansing is provided through a study of the Word of God.

Salvation begins at the cross, but it certainly does not end there. At the altar the priests were justified once for all on the basis of the shed blood. But at the laver, they are to be repeatedly cleansed from the defilement of the world day by day and hour by hour. The altar, therefore speaks of justification, but the laver speaks of the sanctifying power of the Word of God. Our constant contact with the world demands a daily washing by the Word. We need to read it, study it and meditate on it, so it will reveal our defilement. Then we can confess our sin and be cleansed from it.

At the laver, the sins committed after regeneration by the believer are taken care of. It has to do with the defilement after the penalty of sin has been paid. Remember, there was no floor in the tabernacle and from the dirt on their feet, and the necessity of washing their hands from handling the sacrifices, there was a continual cleansing at the laver. The hands speak of their work, and feet suggest their walk. As long as we are here on the earth, we are in the world and stand in constant need of cleansing.

Hebrews 10:22 strikingly connects the cleansing by the blood of the altar and the washing of water at the laver. It reads: "Let us draw near with a true heart in full assurance of faith, having our hearts sprinkled from an evil conscience (the application of the blood at the altar), and our bodies washed with pure water (the cleansing at the laver)." First, the conscience is purged by the sprinkling of the blood; and then the cleansing by the water, which is the Word.

An explanation of this principle is found in John 13 concerning foot-washing. When the Lord came to Peter to wash his feet, Peter said, "Thou shalt never wash my feet." Jesus answered, "If I wash thee not, thou hast no part with me" (verse 8). The word for "part" has the idea of fellowship or partnership in activity. Peter wanted to maintain fellowship, therefore, he said "Not my feet only, but also my hands and my head" (verse 9). Jesus answered, "He that is washed (bathed *louo*) needeth not save to wash (wash *nipto*) his feet, but is clean every whit: and ye are clean, but not all" (verse 10). The first word for washed is *louo*, and means to "bathe all over." The second word is *nipto*, and means "to wash just a part of the body." He was clean every whit by the new birth, but the feet, which speaks of his walk, comes in contact with the earth and needs the daily cleansing.

This action speaks to us of the fact that while we are saved and justified and are in Christ, we, nevertheless, are still in this world of defilement and of sin. We are constantly exposed to the defilements of the world and the flesh. We are subjected to sin in our business life, our social life, our personal life and even in our religious life. It is virtually impossible for a Christian not to be defiled by sin daily. But the Lord knew all about this and the weaknesses of the flesh and has made provision for our continual cleansing. We may come as often as we are defiled. "If we confess our sins, he is faithful and just to forgive us our sins, and to cleanse us from all unrighteousness" (1 John 1:9).

# CHAPTER NINE

# THE CANDLESTICK,
# THE LIGHT OF THE
# WORLD

And thou shalt make a candlestick [of] pure gold: [of] beaten work shall the candlestick be made: his shaft, and his branches, his bowls, his knops, and his flowers, shall be of the same.

And six branches shall come out of the sides of it; three branches of the candlestick out of the one side, and three branches of the candlestick out of the other side:

Three bowls made like unto almonds, [with] a knop and a flower in one branch; and three bowls made like almonds in the other branch, [with] a knop and a flower: so in the six branches that come out of the candlestick.

And in the candlestick [shall be] four bowls made like unto almonds, [with] their knops and their flowers.

And [there shall be] a knop under two branches of the same, and a knop under two branches of the same, and a knop under two branches of the same, according to the six branches that proceed out of the candlestick.

Their knops and their branches shall be of the same: all it [shall be] one beaten work [of] pure gold.

And thou shalt make the seven lamps thereof: and they shall light the lamps thereof, that they may give light over against it.

And the tongs thereof, and the snuffdishes thereof, [shall be of] pure gold.

[Of] a talent of pure gold shall he make it, with all these vessels.

And look that thou make [them] after their pattern, which was shewed thee in the mount.

**Exodus 25:31-40; Cf. Exodus 37:17-24**

# THE CANDLESTICK,
# THE LIGHT OF THE WORLD

The golden lamp stand, also known as the candlestick, was one of the most beautiful pieces of the tabernacle furnishings. The details of its construction are found in Exodus 25:31-40.

Notice, the lamp stand was made of a block of gold weighing one talent. A talent is equivalent to one hundred twenty-five pounds troy weight. At the present price of gold at $407.00 per troy ounce, the value of the lamp stand in weight of gold would be $610,500.00. This is not to mention the value of the workmanship. With the fluctuating price of gold, the value of the candlestick could sometimes exceed one million dollars! It was the most elaborate of all the vessels of the sanctuary as to its workmanship, being richly ornamented.

## What It Looked Like

A description of its construction begins with the "shaft." The shaft was the base. Protruding out of the base upright was a "branch." This branch could also be called a "stem." Branching out from this central stem at regular intervals were three pairs of side branches opposite of each other, adding up to six branches in all. These six side branches along with the main branch or stem made a total of seven branches.

The candlestick was decorated with "bowls, knops and flowers." The "bowl" was shaped like an "almond." Some translations use the word "calyx" in the place of bowl. Calyx is a botanical term in use today, and it is the leaf-like covering of a flower. It has a cup or bowl shape. From this we conclude that the calyxes of the almond flower is the design that was in mind. The "flowers" speak for themselves. The "knops" or "knob" is rendered "ball." The general appearance of the candlestick would thus be a golden almond bush with buds, flowers and fruit. On the main stem or branch, there were four such ornamentations. Proceeding out of the three of them were the side branches. On each of the side branches were three of these ornaments. In all, there were twenty-two of these "bowls, knops and flowers" on the candlestick.

In all fairness, it must be added that many authors interpret the "bowls, knops and flowers" differently. All agree the "bowls" are almonds obviously, since the Scripture so states. Some understand the "knops" to be pomegranates. The Septuagint renders the "flowers" simply as "lilies." These are not unpopular positions for many authors accept them. It is still the opinion of this writer that the "bowls, knops and flowers" answer to the buds, blossoms and fruit of the almond tree, and further reasoning will be offered later.

Fixed to the top of each branch was a lamp. There were seven lamps on the candlestick. Although the lamp stand is referred to as a candlestick, it was not a candle holder as we commonly think of one today. The light was produced by lamps burning olive oil rather than wax candles.

The size of the candlestick is not given in the Bible description, but Jewish tradition assigns it a height of about five feet and a breadth of about three and one-half feet. The lamps traditionally were believed to hold slightly less than a pint of oil.

The candlestick was probably the most skillful and ornamented item in the tabernacle. It was not cast in a mold, nor made of wood and overlaid with gold, neither was it made in sections and assembled. It was beaten into its form and beauty out of a solid block of gold (Ex. 25:31). The skillful ability of Bezaleel, having been "filled, with the spirit of God, ... in all manner of workmanship," has never been matched by even the greatest artists in the world (Ex. 31:2-6).

## The Accessories

The accessories included the "tongs" and "snuffdishes." The word "tongs" in Exodus 25:38 is also translated "snuffers." These tongs were used for dressing the wicks of the lamps. These tongs may or may not be the same tongs used to handle the coals of the altar of incense (Isa. 6:6). The Hebrew word translated "snuffdishes" is so translated only in connection with the candlestick. The same word is translated "censer" or "firepan" in every other place. "Snuffers" and "snuffdishes" are so translated being more apparently in unison with the vessel with which they were connected. Not mentioned here, but elsewhere, were "oil vessels" (Num. 4:9). These too, were probably made of gold.

"Oil for the light" is one of the items directed to be brought by the Israelites as a contribution for the tabernacle (Ex. 25:6). "And thou shalt command the children of Israel, that they bring thee pure oil olive beaten for the light, to cause the lamp to burn always" (Ex. 27:20; Cf. Lev. 24:2). The olives were not put into a press, but were beaten by hand.

The instructions for the moving of the golden candlestick are given in Numbers 4:9-10:

> And they shall take a cloth of blue, and cover the candlestick of the light, and his lamps, and his tongs, and his snuffdishes, and all the oil vessels thereof, wherewith they minister unto it:
> And they shall put it and all the vessels thereof within a covering of badgers' skins, and shall put it upon a bar.

The candlestick and accessories were wrapped in a linen cloth dyed blue, and then covered with badgers' skins. The blue cloth suggests heavenly origin and that the light of the candlestick is from Heaven. The badger's skins were both a protection from the elements and yet indicated Christ as He appeared in the eyes of men with "no form nor comeliness." As with the other items covered with the badgers' skins, their real beauty and purpose is not seen by the human eye.

The candlestick and accessories were appropriately wrapped and set on a "bar." The Hebrew word translated "bar" is obscure and the best meaning we can ascertain is that it is a "pole" or "shaft." However it was shaped, it was used to transport the candlestick and accessories and was probably carried as was the other pieces of furniture. After the lamp stand and accessories were placed on the bar, they were all covered with badgers' skins.

The candlestick was set in the Holy Place on the south side (Ex. 40:24; 26:35). Likely, the branches ran parallel to the walls. Just imagine the beauty! The ceiling, the front entrance and the vail were visible with colors of blue, purple and red on white linen. The walls on two sides and the furniture were all polished gold. With the light of the lamps glimmering against the golden walls, the sight must have been beautiful!

There is a lack of detail regarding the activity of the priests around the candlestick. The trimming of the wicks and filling of the lamps was associated with the burning of incense at the morning and evening sacrifices. Exodus 30:7-8 gives the most information on the subject. It says:

And Aaron shall burn thereon sweet incense every morning: when he dresseth the lamps, he shall burn incense upon it.

And when Aaron lighteth the lamps at even, he shall burn incense upon it, a perpetual incense before the LORD throughout your generations.

## The Burning of the Lamp

The evidence seems to indicate that the lamps of the candlestick were burning only from the evening sacrifice to the morning sacrifice. Notice these instructions regarding the purpose of the oil: "And thou shalt command the children of Israel, that they bring thee pure oil olive beaten for the light, to cause the lamp to burn always" (Ex. 27:20). But also notice: "Aaron and his sons shall order it from evening to morning before the LORD" (Ex. 27:21; Cf. Lev. 24:2-3).

Admittedly, there is one major problem with this position. The question is raised, how the priests could see to officiate during those hours the lamps were not burning. No reasonable answer is offered, but neither is there a reasonable explanation of the passages that so declare that it was burning from evening to morning. Jewish tradition claims the lamps were not burning between the morning and evening hours and in the second Temple, additional lamps were added to provide lighting for those hours. This is only one of many unanswered questions concerning the tabernacle. This presents a problem because there was activity in the Holy Place and sometimes in the Holy of Holies during these hours.

The hours under consideration would be from about 9:00 a.m. in the morning to about 3:00 p.m. in the afternoon. These are the exact hours that Jesus hung on the cross. During three of the hours Jesus hung on the cross there was darkness throughout the land. We are made to wonder if there is significance and we are still in the dark. This may indicate the importance of the light. "Yet a little while is the light with you. Walk while ye have the light, lest darkness come upon you: for he that walketh in darkness knoweth not whither he goeth. While ye have light, believe in the light, that ye may be the children of light" (John 12:35-36).

The purpose of the golden candlestick was more than merely to provide light for the priests to move about. It was to reveal. It revealed the table of shewbread, the altar of incense and the cherubim on the linen covering and the vail. The value and the meaning of the other objects in the Holy Place were illuminated by the lamp stand. Perhaps no other object associated with the tabernacle has so much quantity and variety of meaning as does this lamp stand.

The fact that the candlestick was made from a block of gold and beaten into shape has more meaning than merely a method of fabrication. And the oil from the olives had to be extracted by human beating rather than by an olive press. The beating of the metal lamp stand and the olives doubtless finds its final meaning in the beating and bruising of the Lord Jesus Christ. `Yet it pleased the LORD to bruise him" (Isa. 53:10). "He was wounded for our transgressions, he was bruised for our iniquities" (Isa. 53:5).

We are already familiar with the fact that gold is a symbol of divine glory. The deity of our Lord, therefore, seems to be emphasized in the gold. It may be mere conjecture, but the Triune God seemingly comes out in the symbolism of the candlestick. The gold signifies God the Father. The light represents God the Son. And the oil suggests God the Holy Ghost.

## Jesus is the Light of the World

The light of the candlestick is a perfect, fitting and divine symbol of our Lord Jesus Christ. It is written:

"That was the true Light, which lighteth every man that cometh into the world." (John 1:9).

"Then spake Jesus again unto them, saying, I am the light of the world: he that followeth me shall not walk in darkness, but shall have the light of life." (John 8:12).

"As long as I am in the world, I am the light of the

world." (John 9:5).

"God is light, and in him is no darkness at all." (1 John 1:5).

In John 8:12, Jesus told the Jews, "I am the light of the world." In the very next verse, the Jews responded "Thou bearest record of thyself; thy record is not true" (John 8:13). When Jesus said He was the light of the world, the Jews called Him a liar. Jesus had some other things to tell them in that same chapter, and in verse 28 He said: "When ye have lifted up the Son of man, then shall ye know that I am he, and that I do nothing of myself; but as my Father hath taught me, I speak these things." The lifting up that Jesus spoke of was His being lifted up on the cross. He was saying in effect that when they lift Him up on the cross, that His Father would show them that He was the light of the world.

## Darkness Over the Earth

They did, in fact, lift Jesus up on the cross. They nailed Him to the cross and for three hours they made mockery of Him. They challenged Him to come down from the cross and they would believe. They mocked, they ridiculed, they cursed, they blasphemed, they derided, they scorned. For three hours they were relentless in their verbal attacks. Then something happened. God turned out the light. Luke's record says: "And it was about the sixth hour, and there was darkness over all the earth until the ninth hour" (Luke 23:44). It was high noon, on top of a mountain, and God turned out the light. It was black. So black that one could hardly tell which direction was up or down. So black that one lost all sense of direction.

Suddenly, there was a hush over the crowd. You could hear a pin drop. The mountain was silent. The Father hushed the mockery. We could just imagine after a few minutes of silence some old sage Rabbi spoke up and said: "Well, I remember when I was a boy. We had an eclipse of the sun and it got dark." But this was no eclipse of the sun. An eclipse never gets completely black and it only lasts for seconds. This was no eclipse.

Minutes went by. No one was prepared for this. No one had a lamp on the top of a mountain. The three hours of darkness was from high noon to about three o'clock p.m. It was the three brightest hours of the day. No one was prepared for darkness on top of a mountain at high noon. After a while, the people became exhausted and could only sit down in the spot where they had been standing. Fifteen minutes go by, then twenty minutes, then thirty, then an hour.

There is a quiet rumble among the crowd. The people began to ask themselves: "What is happening here? Where has the sun gone? Where is the light? When is there going to be light again?" Another hour goes by. No doubt the tone of the conversation begins to turn toward the person on the middle cross. He said He was the Light of the world. This is a miracle. What is God trying to do? What is God trying to tell us? And another hour goes by.

It's all over at the end of three hours. The light has only briefly appeared by the time of the death of Jesus on the cross. The evidence was so compelling that the pagan Roman centurion looked upon the lifeless body of Jesus hanging there on the cross and said: "Truly this was the Son of God!" (Matt. 27:54).

God turned out the light to show the world that Jesus is the light of the world. Without Jesus men will walk in eternal darkness.

There were no windows in the tabernacle; thus, there was no natural light whatsoever. So the golden lamp stand pointed to Christ as the only light by which the priests could work and fellowship with God.

## Olive Oil Was The Fuel

Next, we notice the olive oil was the fuel for the candle-stick. Throughout the Scriptures, anointing oil is the divine symbol of the Holy Spirit. Oil was constantly used in anointing or consecrating persons, places and things. The high priest was anointed (Ex. 29:7). The tabernacle and its furniture were anointed (Ex. 40:9). The kings were anointed (2 Sam. 2:4). The prophets were anointed (1 Kings. 19:16). The Lord Jesus Christ is "the Anointed One." The word Messiah means literally the Anointed One." To this certainty, the Lord testified: "The Spirit of the Lord God is upon me; because the LORD hath anoint-ed me" (Isa. 61:1). "God anointed Jesus of Nazareth with the Holy Ghost and with power" (Acts 10:38).

There were seven lamps in the golden candlestick of the tabernacle. There is similarity between this candle-stick and the seven lamps in John's vision around the throne of God. John declares: "And out of the throne pro-ceeded lightnings and thunderings and voices: and there were seven lamps of fire burning before the throne, which are the seven Spirits of God" (Rev. 4:5). The similarity is so plain here that the imagery of the tabernacle candle-stick is that of John's vision of the throne of God. The rela-tionship between God the Father, God the Son and God the Holy Spirit is such that what One does the other does. Jesus Christ is the Holy Spirit, and the Holy Spirit is the Son. It is not unusual for one item to signify in detail both the Spirit and the Son. So while the seven-stemmed lamp stand represents Christ as the light, it also represents the sevenfold Spirit of God. As we think of the lamp stand rep-resenting both Jesus Christ and the Holy Spirit, we must remember that it is impossible to separate the two. The "Spirit of God" and the "Spirit of Christ" are spoken of as the same person in the same passage of scripture (Rom. 8:9).

Some authors compare the lamp stand and its branches to the titles of the Holy Spirit in Isaiah 11:2. It reads: "And the spirit of the LORD shall rest upon him, the spirit of wisdom and understanding, the spirit of counsel and might, the spirit of knowledge and of the fear of the LORD." They make this comparison from the main stem of the candlestick representing the Spirit of the Lord, and the three sets of branches that protrude out from the two sides representing the six descriptive titles. Whether or not the candlestick alludes to the seven aspects of the Spirit in Isaiah 11:2 remains to be seen as a fact. Many writers make the claim. At least, it is an interesting comparison.

## A Misconception

It is not at all unusual for authors to claim that the candlestick represents the church of the Lord Jesus Christ. This theory is based on the church being called golden candlesticks. John had a vision and said "I saw seven golden candlesticks" (Rev. 1:12). The Lord gives John the interpretation of the meaning of the golden candlesticks in Revelation 1:20: "The mystery of the seven stars which thou sawest in my right hand, and the seven golden candlesticks. The seven stars are the angels of the seven churches: and the seven candlesticks which thou sawest are the seven churches."

In all fairness, this is the most popular view. However, in view of the fact that the church was a complete mystery to the Old Testament saint, there is no way that they could have known this. If this be the interpretation, then the Old Testament saint had no idea of what the candlestick represented.

It is the contention of this author that the candlestick of the tabernacle and the light of the seven churches of Asia represented the same thing. That they both represented Jesus Christ as the Light of the world. Two different objects in two different ages, each representing the same thing. This being true, then the Old Testament saint would very well understand the significance of the meaning of the light of the golden menorah. While there is much similarity, one does not represent the other, but rather both represent Jesus Christ. The light of the candlestick was not the true light but was symbolic of the true light. The light of the church only reflects the true light of Jesus Christ.

The commission that was given to John the Baptist was basically the same one that was given to the churches of the Lord. The commission reads: "The same came for a witness, to bear witness of the Light, that all men through him might believe. He was not that Light, but was sent to bear witness of that Light. That was the true Light, which lighteth every man that cometh into the world" (John 1:7-10). Jesus said to His church: "Ye are the light of the world" (Matt. 5:14).

Neither John nor the churches are the true Light. They reflect the true Light as the moon reflects the light of the sun. The golden candlestick in the tabernacle was not the true Light, but was symbolic of the true Light. Thus, the golden candlestick of the tabernacle and the light of the churches are symbolic of the same heavenly Light. The two symbols do not represent each other, but they reflect the same object. Two different objects may represent the same thing and not represent each other. The church is not symbolic of the light bearing of John the Baptist. Therefore, the golden candlestick of the tabernacle does not represent the churches of the Lord.

## The Shape of an Almond Tree?

The golden lamp stand was in the shape of an almond tree, with seven branches, having buds, flowers and fruit upon them. Why an almond tree? The answer will be found with Aaron's rod that budded.

Some of the Israeli leadership began to challenge Aaron's position as High Priest. They came to Moses and said they could do the job as well as Aaron could and who appointed Aaron over them in the first place? God wanted to show all Israel that Aaron was the divinely-designed priest, to silence the murmuring of the children of Israel. Each tribe was to select a representative from their tribe that they would nominate to be High Priest. Naturally, the tribe of Levi chose Aaron. Each man was to bring a rod to the sanctuary with their name inscribed on it. The rods were placed in the tabernacle (Num. 17). "And it came to pass, that on the morrow Moses went into the tabernacle of witness; and, behold, the rod of Aaron for the house of Levi was budded, and brought forth buds, and bloomed blossoms, and yielded almonds" (verse 8).

Eleven of the rods were the same as they were when placed in the tabernacle, but Aaron's rod came to life. During the middle of the night, that dead rod began to sprout out limbs. It put forth buds, blossoms and even had ripe almonds growing out of it. It was God's sign to Israel, who He had chosen to be the High Priest.

When Jesus came on the scene, the Jews came to Him saying: "Master, we would see a sign from thee" (Matt. 12:38). Jesus said: "An evil and adulterous generation seeketh after a sign" (Matt. 12:39). Jesus told them, "You want a sign. I'll give you a sign." So He turned the water to wine, multiplied the loaves and fishes and fed thousands. So He calmed the storm and stilled the seas. Even the elements obeyed His voice. They came to Him and said, "If you are the Son of God, give us a sign and we will believe." So He healed the sick, made the lame to walk, and cleansed the lepers. And they came to Him again and said, "If you are the Son of God, give us a sign and we will believe." So He made the blind to see, the deaf to hear and the dumb to speak. And they came to Him again and said, "If you are the Son of God, give us a sign and we will believe." So He raised men from the dead. He walked up to the tombs of dead men and ordered them to come alive and come forth. Again and again, they came back and said: "If you are the Son of God, give us a sign and we will believe."

So, they nailed Jesus to the cross. They walked by the cross and in mockery said: "Let him now come down from the cross, and we will believe him" (Matt. 27:42). Jesus had said, "You want a sign, I'll give you a sign!" He said: "And there shall no sign be given to it, but the sign of the prophet Jonas: For as Jonas was three days and three nights in the whale's belly; so shall the Son of man be three days and three nights in the heart of the earth." (Matt. 12:39-40). "Jesus answered and said unto them, Destroy this temple, and in three days I will raise it up." (John 2:19).

The reprobate Jews walked by the cross and in mockery dared Jesus to come down from the cross. He said, "I'll do better than that. I'll hang here until I'm dead. I'll let you bury me in a tomb, put over it a great stone and seal it with concrete. I'll let you place a guard to protect it. But, I'll be back!" Now I ask, which would have been more sensational? For Jesus to have stepped down off that cross and walked away in the midst of the people? Or, for Jesus to have hung on the cross until He was dead, buried and then on the third day raise Himself from the dead? It is one thing for a live man to raise another from the dead, but it is entirely a different matter for a dead man to raise himself from the dead.

Let's face facts. Jesus was more powerful dead than the Devil is alive. Jesus had already said: "I lay down my life, that I might take it again. No man taketh it from me, but I lay it down of myself. I have power to lay it down, and I have power to take it again." (John 10:17-18). Jesus had power to give life to that which was dead.

Aaron's rod that budded signified the resurrection of Christ. The rod that was dead and given life represents Christ who is able to give life to that which is dead. Christ overcame death by His own power and is able to give life to those who are dead in trespasses and sins. Resurrection and life, then, is God's proof of the eternal priesthood of His beloved Son. And this seems to be what is set forth in the buds, flowers and fruit of the almond upon the branches of the golden candlestick, The Hebrew word for almonds means "wakeful," or "hastener." It has been given that name because it is the earliest of the trees to awaken after the winter, putting forth its buds in January.

Now I ask, what is the worst piece of real estate on earth? The answer is clear, a cemetery. A cemetery is the worst piece of property on earth. Every community on earth has one or more. It is a necessary evil. We hate cemeteries because they rob us of our loved ones. It is the most dreadful place on earth. We cannot pass a cemetery holding the grave of a loved one without feeling deep emotion. Cemeteries greet us at the end of our lives. They are so final. But, beloved, when that trumpet sounds, and there is the shout from heaven and the voice of the archangel, it's over! Every grave holding God's children from one end of the earth to the other will give them up. The most dreadful site on the face of the earth will become the site of the greatest victory for a child of God. Jesus has the power to turn the worst into the best. As fast as the blink of an eye, the cemetery will give up the dead in Christ. And there is no power on earth or in hell that can stop it. Jesus has power to give life to a dead soul and He has power to give life to our dead bodies.

I can see it now. We will come bursting out of those graves with our new bodies on our way to the glories of heaven, and on the way out, we will be inclined to quote a verse from the fifteenth chapter of the book of Second Corinthians .... "O grave, where is thy victory?"

The significance of the decorations on the golden candlestick was an object lesson to the Israelites of the ability of Christ to give life to the dead soul and the resurrection of the dead body from the grave.

# CHAPTER TEN

# BREAD AT THE
# TABLE OF SHEWBREAD

Thou shalt also make a table [of] shittim wood: two cubits [shall be] the length thereof, and a cubit the breadth thereof, and a cubit and a half the height thereof.

And thou shalt overlay it with pure gold, and make thereto a crown of gold round about.

And thou shalt make unto it a border of an hand breadth round about, and thou shalt make a golden crown to the border thereof round about.

And thou shalt make for it four rings of gold, and put the rings in the four corners that [are] on the four feet thereof.

Over against the border shall the rings be for places of the staves to bear the table.

And thou shalt make the staves [of] shittim wood, and overlay them with gold, that the table may be borne with them.

And thou shalt make the dishes thereof, and spoons thereof, and covers thereof, and bowls thereof, to cover withal: [of] pure gold shalt thou make them.

And thou shalt set upon the table shewbread before me alway.

Exodus 25:23-30

# BREAD AT THE
# TABLE OF SHEWBREAD

Immediately across the room from the candlestick was the table of shewbread. God instructed Moses how to build it in Exodus 25:23-30.

The table of shewbread was made of shittim (acacia) wood and was overlaid in pure gold, so the appearance was as solid gold. The table was thirty-six inches (two cubits), in length. It was eighteen inches (one cubit) in breadth or width. And it stood twenty-seven inches (one-half cubits) high.

Around the top of the table was a crown of gold. There was also a "border" around the table. There are different ideas as to how this border was made. The word itself means enclosure, border or rim. There was a second crown of gold around this border. The width of the border was a "hand's breadth" or approximately four inches.

There are two possibilities regarding this border. One is that it is next to the first crown of gold and vertically extends up four inches around the perimeter of the table with a crown of gold around the top. The other possibility is that it extends out horizontally from the table about four inches and has another crown on the outside edge extending up like the first. In either case, as a rim, its purpose was to hold the bread and utensils on the table.

Four rings were made with one on each corner in which the staves would pass through for the method of transporting the table. These staves, like the others, were made of wood and overlaid in gold. The mention of four feet indicate there were legs to the table rather than a box-type build.

The table of shewbread was set in the Holy Place on the north side of the wall or on the right side as the priests entered the room (Ex. 26:35).

## Making the Bread

Instructions for the shewbread are given in Leviticus 24:5-9:

> And thou shalt take fine flour, and bake twelve cakes thereof: two tenth deals shall be in one cake.
>
> And thou shalt set them in two rows, six on a row, upon the pure table before the LORD.
>
> And thou shalt put pure frankincense upon each row, that it may be on the bread for a memorial, even an offering made by fire unto the LORD.
>
> Every sabbath he shall set it in order before the LORD continually, being taken from the children of Israel by an everlasting covenant.
>
> And it shall be Aaron's and his Sons'; and they shall eat it in the holy place: for it is most holy unto him of the offerings of the LORD made by fire by a perpetual statute.

Actually, the shewbread was a meat (meal) offering of which the details of its baking are more fully discussed in Leviticus, chapter two. Particular attention is given here to the shewbread as it pertains to the table.

The bread was called "shewbread," and was made into "cakes." The word shewbread means "bread of face" or "presence bread," suggesting that it was set before the face of God. The word rendered "cakes" is literally "pierced caked," so called because they were pierced or perforated to allow quick and thorough baking and to have possible spiritual meaning.

The twelve cakes were made of "fine flour," representing the twelve tribes of Israel. The amount of flour used for each loaf was "two tenth deals." A deal was an ephah, and "two tenth deals" was slightly more than two quarts.

There were "two rows, six in a row" of bread upon the table. The meaning of the two rows of bread is debatable. Some claim there were two rows of bread laying side by side on the table. Others contend, based upon Jewish tradition, that there were two "piles" of bread, each having six loaves in a stack. The language does not settle the issue. The word translated "row" also means "pile" and "heap." The strongest argument in favor of the piles of bread concerns the amount of bread and accessories required to be placed on such a small table. Each student must decide for himself the arrangement he thinks best.

It was the duty of the priests each Sabbath day to place fresh or hot bread on the table (1 Sam. 21:6). The old cakes were then eaten by the priests in the Holy Place (Lev. 24:5-9). The Kohathites had charge of the preparation of the shewbread in the tabernacle (1 Chron. 9:32). It was this bread that David requested of Ahimelech, the priest, for himself and his men (1 Sam. 21:1-6; Cf. Matt. 12:4).

## Frankincense on the Bread

Upon the two rows of shewbread was placed "frankincense." "And thou shalt put pure frankincense upon each row, that it may be on the bread for a memorial, even an offering made by fire unto the LORD" (Lev. 24:7). The Hebrew word *lebonah*, translated "frankincense," is derived from a root word signifying "to be white." The word "Lebanon" is derived from the same root word. The Hebrew word for the "moon" is also from the same root word because of its silvery whiteness. Frankincense is a remarkable white gum taken from certain trees.

Opinions concerning the placement of the frankincense are varied. Some place the frankincense in a vessel and put it upon the stacks or piles of bread, while others pour it out upon the bread as icing upon a cake. Some authors say when it is warmed or burned that it produces a sweet, pleasant odor. Some say that it has a bitter taste when eaten. The clue has to be in the word "put," translated from the Hebrew *nathan*. In Leviticus 14:18 it is translated "pour" in the phrase: "And the remnant of the oil that is in the priest's hand he shall pour upon the head of him that is to be cleansed." Since there is no indication of a container holding the frankincense, and since the word "put" is also translated "pour," it is the conclusion of this author that the frankincense was poured upon the bread as icing would be upon a cake.

## Accessories to the Table

The accessories to the table of shewbread consisted of dishes, spoons, bowls and cups. "And thou shalt make the dishes thereof, and spoons thereof, and covers thereof, and bowls thereof, to cover withal: of pure gold shalt thou make them" (Ex. 25:29). All the accessories were made of pure gold.

Why all the accessories? And what purpose did they serve? The dishes are most commonly believed to have held the loaves of shewbread. The dishes are translated "chargers" in Numbers chapter seven, but the meaning is the same. The spoons, bowls and cups require a closer examination.

The word "spoon" comes from a Hebrew word meaning "palm of hand, pan, spoon, or dish." The indication is that it is similar to our "spoon" or "dipper." The purpose of this spoon is not clear. Perhaps it was used to dip and pour the frankincense upon the bread.

Most authors suggest the spoon was used for incense. In Numbers chapter seven, twelve golden spoons were presented by the princes, filled with incense for the use of the sanctuary. These spoons are not necessarily the same as on the table of shewbread, as the silver chargers holding the shewbread were certainly not the same. The point is that the spoons were used for incense, and there is no other stated purpose for the spoons on the table. Since these spoons were on the table, it is this author's thinking that they had to do with the table of shewbread in some manner especially since the altar of incense had its own accessories.

## The Drink Offering

The two remaining sets of vessels attached to the table were "covers" and "bowls." Here the question occurs as before, to what end were these vessels kept at the table of shewbread. The King James' Version uses the following language: "and covers thereof, and bowls thereof, to cover withal" (Ex. 25:29). The American Standard Version uses this language: "and the flagons thereof, and the bowls thereof, wherewith to pour out."

This phrase is quite interesting, and gives us far more information than the English translation indicates. The first word "covers" and the term "to cover withal" are entirely different words. The first word "covers" is *qasvah* and means "jug" or "jar." The second term "to cover withal" is *nasak* and means "to pour out."

Again in Numbers 4:7, the following English translation is offered: "and covers to cover withal." And again, the two words for cover are different words. The term "to cover withal" in most every other place is translated "drink-offering." This passage could literally be translated: "jars of the drink-offering." There is no explanation that can be offered why the expression "to cover withal" was not translated "drink-offering."

Now, to consider the "bowl." The word bowl is from a Hebrew root word meaning "sacrificial bowl" and "pour out." The apparent idea is that this bowl was used to actually pour out the drink-offering. The jar appears to be a container holding the wine (drink-offering). From the jar, the wine was poured into the bowl by measure. And, from the bowl, the wine was poured out as a drink-offering.

Not only do the terms themselves lend evidence that there was a drink-offering associated with the table of shewbread, but there are other suggestions as well. There is no direct passage in the English that so declares, but the evidence is obvious that the jars and bowls on the table were used for the drink-offering.

The drink-offering was always associated with the meat (meal) offering (Num. 15:1-10). The bread on the table of shewbread was a meat-offering (Lev. 2:1-16).

Authors have been curious as to what happened to the wine. The Law strictly forbade any priest from drinking "wine nor strong drink" when working in the tabernacle (Lev. 10:9). Some writers feel it was poured out at the base of the brazen altar or on it. Exodus 30:9 forbids it being poured out at the altar of incense.

However, Numbers 28:7 speaks of it being poured out at the Holy Place: "In the holy place shalt thou cause the strong wine to be poured unto the LORD for a drink-offering." The probability is that the wine was poured out at the base of the table of shewbread.

## Traveling With The Table

The provision for transporting the table of shewbread is stated in Numbers 4:7-8:

> And upon the table of shewbread they shall spread a cloth of blue, and put thereon the dishes, and the spoons, and the bowls, and covers to cover withal: and the continual bread shall be thereon:
> And they shall spread upon them a cloth of scarlet, and cover the same with a covering of badgers' skins, and shall put in the staves thereof.

First, the table was cleared of the bread, wine and utensils and then covered with a blue linen cloth. The items were placed on the blue cloth and wrapped together. A scarlet cloth was then put in place. The covering of badgers' skins was added. The staves were put in place and the table was ready for moving. The table was the only piece of furniture that was wrapped in a scarlet cloth. Scarlet is the crimson color that symbolizes the shed blood of Jesus. Perhaps the blue cloth represents the bread that came down from Heaven, and the scarlet represents the wine which symbolizes the shed blood of Christ. And again, the badgers' skins are only visible to the human eye indicating the true understanding is revealed only to those with spiritual sight.

## The Ritual at the Table

The Sabbath was a very busy day for the priests. In addition to their regular and special duties, the table of shewbread received special attention. The priests would enter the Holy Place with twelve fresh and hot loaves of bread. The old bread would be removed and the new would be placed on the table, and then the priest would pour frankincense upon the bread. Another priest would pour the wine from the jar into the bowl and supposedly poured it around at the base of the table. A new jar of wine would then be placed on the table. With this done, the priests would gather around and eat the bread taken from the table. If any of the bread was not eaten and left until the next morning, it was to be burned (Ex. 29:33-34).

As indicated previously, the acacia wood speaks of the humanity of Christ. However, it was overlaid with pure gold, which speaks of the deity of Christ. The combination of the two reminds us that Jesus Christ was the God-man. Although Christ took upon Himself human flesh, He was also God. The accessories being of pure gold give emphasis to Christ being God.

The two crowns of gold served more purpose than a mere ridge to restrain the items on the top and to beautify it. The crowns speak of "Jesus, crowned with glory and honour" (Heb. 2:9). No longer the crown of thorns, but the victor's crown now adorns His head. One day He will appear as the "KING OF KINGS, AND LORD OF LORDS" (Rev. 19:16). For this purpose, "God also hath highly exalted him, and given him a name which is above every name: that at the name of Jesus every knee should bow, of things in heaven, and things in earth, and things under the earth" (Phil. 2:9-10).

## Jesus is the Bread of Life

The bread on the table was a beautiful symbol of Christ's body. It is not difficult to interpret the meaning of the shewbread in the light of the New Testament. Jesus stated:

> Our fathers did eat manna in the desert; as it is written, He gave them bread from heaven to eat.
> Then Jesus said unto them, Verily, verily, I say unto you, Moses gave you not that bread from heaven; but my Father giveth you the true bread from heaven.
> For the bread of God is he which cometh down from heaven, and giveth life unto the world.
> Then said they unto him, Lord, evermore give us this bread.
> And Jesus said unto them, I am the bread of life: he that cometh to me shall never hunger; and he that believeth on me shall never thirst.
>
> John 6:31-35

> I am that bread of life.
> Your fathers did eat manna in the wilderness, and are dead.
> This is the bread which cometh down from heaven,

that a man may eat thereof, and not die.

I am the living bread which came down from heaven: if any man eat of this bread, he shall live for ever: and the bread that I will give is my flesh, which I will give for the life of the world.

John 6:48-51

The flour, a product of the earth, had not only to be ground in the mill but sieved, tested and proved to be "fine" flour before it could be used for shewbread. Jesus not only passed through the mill of suffering, He was tested and proved as "fine" and perfect in character. The bread was the result of a process of death and suffering, for the wheat had been harvested, ground to powder and baked in a hot oven. So the Son of God had been ground beneath the millstones of the cross and had passed through the agonizing test of the oven-like heat of the wrath of God against the sin He represented.

## No Leaven in the Bread

The bread was also to be unleavened. Leaven is used in the Bible as a symbol of sin. Since the bread was unleavened, it was a marvelous symbol of the pure and sinless Christ. Here is the verdict:

Pilate said: "I find no fault in this man." (Luke 23:4).

Pilate's wife said: "Have thou nothing to do with that just man." (Matthew 27:19).

Judas said: "I have sinned in that I have betrayed the innocent blood." (Matthew 27:4).

The malefactor said: "This man hath done nothing amiss." (Luke 23:41).

The centurion said: "Certainly this was a righteous man." (Luke 23:47).

God said: "My beloved Son, in whom I am well pleased" (Matthew 17:5).

He was indeed "Holy, harmless, undefiled, separate

from sinners." (Hebrews 7:26).

There were twelve loaves representing the twelve tribes of Israel. There was bread enough for everyone. The significance is that the "true bread" is sufficient for all those who wish to partake.

The wine of the drink-offering depicts the blood of Jesus. This too is interpreted in light of the New Testament. In concluding the Passover feast and the institution of the Lord's Supper, Jesus raised the cup of wine before the disciples and said: "Drink ye all of it; for this is my blood of the new testament, which is shed for many for the remission of sins" (Matt. 26:27-28). This He did immediately after He broke the bread and gave it to His disciples to eat while telling them that it represented His broken body. Paul quoted the words of Jesus when he said: "For as often as ye eat this bread, and drink this cup, ye do shew the Lord's death till he come" (1 Cor. 11:26; Cf. verses 24-25).

In this case, the wine was not drunk, but was poured out at the base of the table. This clearly shows the blood of Christ shed at the base of the cross.

No doubt, it was to this table of shewbread containing the bread and wine that Jesus alluded to in John 6:53-56:

> Then Jesus said unto them, Verily, verily, I say unto you, Except ye eat the flesh of the Son of man, and drink his blood, ye have no life in you.
>
> Whoso eateth my flesh, and drinketh my blood, hath eternal life; and I will raise him up at the last day.
>
> For my flesh is meat indeed, and my blood is drink indeed.
>
> He that eateth my flesh, and drinketh my blood, dwelleth in me, and I in him.

We do not literally eat His body and drink His blood. When we do eat and drink the substance becomes a part of our body. When we receive Jesus into our heart and soul in salvation, He literally becomes a part of us. The physical eating and drinking is symbolical of spiritually receiving the broken body and shed blood into our lives.

The table of shewbread was also the center of fellowship in the priestly family. Around this table the priests would gather and eat the bread in fellowship. Here the priests came together and found their unity.

If we desire to know a friend more intimately, it is customary to ask them to our home for a meal or refreshments. To come together on the basis of the broken body and shed blood is to come together for the greatest reason in the world. It is appropriate that the New Testament ordinance of the Lord's Supper be called "communion." The nearer Christians get to Christ, the nearer they get to one another.

# CHAPTER ELEVEN

# PRAYER AT THE
# ALTAR OF INCENSE

And thou shalt make an altar to burn incense upon: [of] shittim wood shalt thou make it.

A cubit [shall be] the length thereof, and a cubit the breadth thereof; foursquare shall it be: and two cubits [shall be] the height thereof: the horns thereof [shall be] of the same.

And thou shalt overlay it with pure gold, the top thereof, and the sides thereof round about, and the horns thereof; and thou shalt make unto it a crown of gold round about.

And two golden rings shalt thou make to it under the crown of it, by the two corners thereof, upon the two sides of it shalt thou make [it]; and they shall be for places for the staves to bear it withal.

And thou shalt make the staves [of] shittim wood, and overlay them with gold.

And thou shalt put it before the vail that [is] by the ark of the testimony, before the mercy seat that [is] over the testimony, where I will meet with thee.

And Aaron shall burn thereon sweet incense every morning: when he dresseth the lamps, he shall burn incense upon it.

And when Aaron lighteth the lamps at even, he shall burn incense upon it, a perpetual incense before the LORD throughout your generations.

Ye shall offer no strange incense thereon, nor burnt sacrifice, nor meat offering; neither shall ye pour drink offering thereon.

And Aaron shall make an atonement upon the horns of it once in a year with the blood of the sin offering of atonements: once in the year shall he make atonement upon it throughout your generations: it [is] most holy unto the LORD.

**Exodus 30:1-10; Exodus 37:25-28**

# PRAYER AT THE ALTAR OF INCENSE

An appraisal of the altar of incense must begin with the instructions for its construction as found in Exodus 30:1-10. The altar of incense was definitely the smallest piece of furniture. This fact does not make it any more or less important than the rest. The altar was eighteen inches (one cubit) square and thirty-six inches (two cubits) high. It was made of shittim (acacia) wood and overlaid with pure gold. A crown of gold was fashioned around the top probably to help contain the coals of fire as well as to decorate. There is no number equated to the horns, but it likely had four as did the altar of burnt-offering. The most plausible location of the horns was in the four corners.

The instructions call for "two golden rings" placed under the crown of gold through which the staves would fit in order to transport the altar. This detail has been interpreted several ways. Since the altar was small and only two rings were mentioned, it is commonly believed that only one ring was needed on each side to adequately carry the altar. Some put the rings in the corners of the altar opposite each other. Others put them in the center of two opposite sides. On the other hand, some designers feel the intent of the language meant that there were two rings on one side which made a total of four rings, and that each stave passed through two rings. The four ring idea would certainly have greater stability than the two in transporting even though it was not a large piece of furniture. Whatever design one thinks best is admittedly personal preference.

## Recipe For Incense

The particulars for making the incense are found in Exodus 30:34-38:

> And the LORD said unto Moses, Take unto thee sweet spices, stacte, and onycha, and galbanum; these sweet spices with pure frankincense: of each shall there be a like weight:
>
> And thou shalt make it a perfume, a confection after the art of the apothecary, tempered together, pure and holy:
>
> And thou shalt beat some of it very small, and put of it before the testimony in the tabernacle of the congregation, where I will meet with thee: it shall be unto you most holy.
>
> And as for the perfume which thou shalt make, ye shall not make to yourselves according to the composition thereof: it shall be unto thee holy for the LORD.
>
> Whosoever shall make like unto that, to smell thereto, shall even be cut off from his people.

Three sweet spices are here mentioned, "stacte, onycha and galbanum," the names of which nowhere else occur in Scripture. Exactly what these spices were cannot be determined in absolutes. There is some agreement among researchers as to what they probably were. The "stacte" is believed to be a sweet gum from a specie of the styrax plant. The "onycha" is believed to be the shell from a mollusk shell-fish from which the name comes. When the shell is ground up it yields a perfume. "Galbanum" is believed to be a resinous gum obtained from a shrub. This gum is said to have a naturally disagreeable odor, but when added to other ingredients it gives strength and persistence. The fourth ingredient was "frankincense" and it is the same as the frankincense on the table of shewbread. In brief, it is a white resin, which is very fragrant when burnt.

There was a definite command concerning the use of the altar of incense and the incense allowed upon it. "Ye shall offer no strange incense thereon, nor burnt-sacrifice, nor meat-offering; neither shall ye pour drink-offering thereon" (Ex. 30:9).

## Accessories to the Altar of Incense

The utensils which were necessarily used in the ministry of the golden altar of incense are not specifically mentioned. "Tongs" are mentioned elsewhere in regard to taking the coals from off the altar (Isa. 6:6). There is a mention of "instruments" in connection with the packing and transporting of the altar. These orders are found in Numbers 4:11-12, which state:

> And upon the golden altar they shall spread a cloth of blue, and cover it with a covering of badgers' skins, and shall put to the staves thereof:
> And they shall take all the instruments of ministry, wherewith they minister in the sanctuary, and put them in a cloth of blue, and cover them with a covering of badgers' skins, and shall put them on a bar.

## Traveling with the Altar of Incense

The altar was wrapped in a linen cloth dyed blue and then covered with badgers' skins. With the staves passing through the rings in the side, it was moved around. The instruments associated with the altar were also wrapped in blue linen cloth and covered with badgers' skins. These were put on a "bar" like the candlestick was put on. The word bar means "pole" or "staff." The small size of the altar probably necessitated the extra bar to carry the utensils.

## Ritual at the Altar of Incense

Each morning, at the third hour (nine o'clock in the morning), the priests would enter the Holy Place and trim the lamp stand. At the same time, they would offer incense on the altar. Each evening (three o'clock in the afternoon), the priests would enter the Holy Place again and light the candlestick and once again burn incense on the altar. Before the incense would be burned, the old coals were taken off the altar, and new hot coals from the brazen altar were brought in and placed there.

When the Lord appeared to Zacharias about the birth of John, he was burning incense in the Temple (Luke 1:8-10). While Zacharias was burning incense inside the Temple "the whole multitude of the people were praying without." Recognizing the significance of the offering of incense, the people were drawn to spend time in prayer.

The altar of incense was strategically located in the Holy Place immediately in front of the vail. Exodus 40:5 states its position: "And thou shalt set the altar of gold for the incense before the ark of the testimony." Its position was in the direct line of approach to the ark and the mercy seat.

## Another Altar

Of the three articles of furniture in the Holy Place, the altar of incense was unquestionably the most significant and important. This is indicated not only by its position between the other two, immediately in front of the entrance to the Holy of Holies, but also by its designation as an altar.

The fact that the blood was sprinkled on the mercy seat and smeared on the horns of the altar of incense establishes an essential relation between it and the altar and the mercy seat. The other two articles of furniture were offshoots, as it were, of the altar of incense as the position on either side indicated.

The altar of incense in the tabernacle holds the same position as the altar did in John's vision of the throne in Heaven. "And another angel came and stood at the altar, having a golden censer; and there was given unto him much incense that he should offer it with the prayers of all saints upon the golden altar which was before the throne" (Rev. 8:3). The ark of the covenant and mercy seat symbolically represented God's throne, and the altar of incense was to be set "before the ark of the testimony" (Ex. 40:5).

The difference between the two is the vail that hung between them, but now there is no vail seeing it has been rent in twain and we have boldness to enter into His presence. Prior to the rending of the vail, whenever the high priest entered into the Most Holy Place, he would carry a censer of coals taken from the altar of incense and offer incense before the ark and mercy seat (Lev. 16:12-13). In the book of Hebrews, the apostle Paul makes a contrast between the "first" tabernacle and the "second" tabernacle. He mentioned the similarities between the tabernacle of Moses and the things of Heaven it represented. In enumerating the various articles of furniture in the first tabernacle, the altar of incense is omitted, and instead we have the "golden censer" in the Holy of Holies. The account reads: "And after the second veil, the tabernacle which is called the Holiest of all; which had the golden censer, and the ark of the covenant overlaid round about with gold, wherein was the golden pot that had manna, and Aaron's rod that budded, and the tables of the covenant" (Heb. 9:3-4).

The epistle to the Hebrews contemplates the vail as rent through the perfect sacrifice of Christ, and the "way into the holiest" is now manifest, whereas under the Law the vail separated. The altar was not in the Most Holy Place; yet it is evident that worship in its fullest sense is directly in the presence of God.

The vail separated the altar of incense and the throne of God. If the incense represented the prayers of the saints of God, then it is clear that the presence of the vail hindered these prayers. Why? Because of our sins, we did not have free access to the presence of God. All our prayers were brought unto the Father by Jesus Christ. But since the vail is rent, we now, by virtue of His death, have free access to the very throne of God through prayer. We can now go directly to the Father because we have been made priests of God through the sacrifice and rending of Jesus Christ. "Unto him that loved us, and washed us from our sins in his own blood, and hath made us kings and priests unto God and his Father" (Rev. 1:5-6).

The altar was made of wood and overlaid with pure gold. It is again a picture of the Lord Jesus in His humanity, the gold speaking of His unchangeable deity.

The first altar had no crown and pictured Christ in His humiliation. The second had a crown and pictured Christ in His exultation. The brazen altar was the place of suffering and typifies Christ as Savior. The golden altar was the place of triumph and typifies Christ as the mediator.

The horns, as we have seen already in the brazen altar, speak of power and strength. Being on the altar of incense, they must indicate the great power and strength of prayer. The horns pointing to all four directions suggest the universal accessibility of all men to approach the Lord in prayer; none are excluded. Prayer has the power to accomplish things that never could be performed by human might. If we have the "faith as a grain of mustard seed," we could remove mountains. James says, "Is any among you afflicted? let him pray" (James 5:13). He tells us further that "the prayer of faith shall save the sick, and the Lord shall raise him up" (verse 15). The power of prayer is summed up in James 5:16: "The effectual fervent prayer of a righteous man availeth much."

## Jesus Prays For Us!

The incense on the altar is symbolic of prayer. This conclusion is interpreted by Scripture. "Let my prayer be set forth before thee as incense" (Psalm 141:2). A scene in Heaven speaks of "golden vials full of odours (literally incense), which are the prayers of saints" (Rev. 5:8).

Incense on the altar was offered by the priest. The golden altar represented the Lord Jesus Christ. The priest represented Christ as mediator. And since prayer is seen in the incense, the altar of incense specifically portrays Christ as representing the saints before the throne of God. "For Christ is not entered into the holy places made with hands, which are the figures of the true; but into heaven itself, now to appear in the presence of God for us" (Heb. 9:24). "He ever liveth to make intercession for them" (Heb. 7:25). "I pray for them: I pray not for the world, but for them which thou hast given me; for they are thine" (John 17:9).

What an amazing fact it is that He who is the Master of Heaven and earth prays for us! It may not be that He is praying for just the things we wish, nor even such things as we dream, but the fact of His praying demonstrates His interest in, and His grace and care for us.

If we would only believe that He is praying for us! What would it matter that we are in the midst of a tempest and a storm if we believed He was praying for us? What would it matter if we stood with hands of helplessness if we knew that He was praying for us? What would it matter if our plans were shattered if we knew that He was interceding for us? If we would only realize that in the midst of the troubles of life, Jesus Christ our Savior is yonder in Heaven praying for us. How could we possibly fail with that happening?

How often have we escaped sickness, disease, the assault of circumstances and sudden death because He has prayed for us! Just how often He has interceded on our behalf and brought the special providence of God over us, we shall never know until the record of it is read thus when we stand fact to face with Him in glory.

What a beautiful picture this is. The Lord Jesus Himself prays for us, and then He takes our prayers and presents them before God in the fragrance of His own character. Without His intercession, not a single petition of ours would ever ascend to the court of Heaven.

The intercession of Christ on our behalf rests wholly and becomes effective in the sacrifice of Christ on the cross. The horns of the altar of incense were stained once a year with the blood of atonement from the brazen altar. "And Aaron shall make an atonement upon the horns of it once in a year with the blood of the sin-offering" (Ex. 30:10).

Had Jesus not died and met the claims of divine justice against us, He could not intercede for us. Had He not offered Himself as a sacrifice, He could not enter that court on our behalf. The sacrifice was made on the brazen altar, but the atonement is complete on the golden altar. "And the bullock for the sin-offering; whose blood was brought in to make atonement in the holy place" (Lev. 16:27).

With this in mind, "Let us therefore come boldly unto the throne of grace, that we may obtain mercy, and find grace to help in time of need" (Heb. 4:16).

# CHAPTER TWELVE

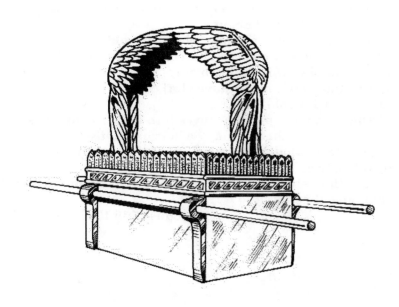

# JUDGMENT AT THE
# ARK OF THE COVENANT

And they shall make an ark [of] shittim wood: two cubits and a half [shall be] the length thereof, and a cubit and a half the breadth thereof, and a cubit and a half the height thereof.

And thou shalt overlay it with pure gold, within and without shalt thou overlay it, and shalt make upon it a crown of gold round about.

And thou shalt cast four rings of gold for it, and put [them] in the four corners thereof; and two rings [shall be] in the one side of it, and two rings in the other side of it.

And thou shalt make staves [of] shittim wood, and overlay them with gold.

And thou shalt put the staves into the rings by the sides of the ark, that the ark may be borne with them.

The staves shall be in the rings of the ark: they shall not be taken from it.

And thou shalt put into the ark the testimony which I shall give thee.

**Exodus 25:10-16; Exodus 37:1-5**

# THE ARK OF THE COVENANT

We have proceeded from the outer court through the Holy Place into the Holy of Holies. In this special room in the tabernacle were the ark of the covenant and the mercy seat. These two items appeared as one piece of furniture. They each have separate significance, but also have purpose as a unit. These ranked the highest in importance of all the furniture of the tabernacle and were the reason the room was called the Holy of Holies.

Moses was not ignorant of the exact instructions for building the ark. He was told how to build it in Exodus 2 5:10-16.

The ark was a chest or box made of shittim (acacia) wood and overlaid on the inside and outside with pure gold. It was hollow on the inside. It was forty-five inches (two and one-half cubits) long; twenty-seven inches (one and one-half cubits) wide; twenty-seven inches (a cubit and one-half) high. The word "half" in the Hebrew comes from a root which means to cut in two.

The position of the ark was most significant. It was placed within the vail in the Holy of Holies. It and the mercy seat were the only items in this Most Holy Place. The presence of the ark and the mercy seat in the Holy of Holies constituted God's throne on the earth and was representative of the throne of God in Heaven.

## Handles In The Ark

Unlike the other pieces of furniture, the staves for carrying the ark were specifically required to remain in the rings at all times. Likely, the staves in the other pieces of furniture were removed when the tabernacle was not on the move, but this was not the case with the ark and the mercy seat. When the ark was finally placed in the sanctuary built by Solomon, the staves were permanently removed (1 Kings 8:8). The instructions for the movement of the ark imply the staves were placed in the ark each time it was moved (Num. 4:4-6). These instructions were given for the first move, and once the staves were placed in the ark, they were not removed until the ark was set in the Temple.

Any Israelite was aware of the purpose of the staves in the ark. Their presence made their purpose all too obvious. There was a time in Israel's history that they became so disobedient that the Lord allowed them to be afflicted by the Philistines for the intended purpose of drawing them back to Himself. The Israelites knew that on a certain day the Philistines were going to attack. They got the bright idea that if they brought the ark of the covenant to the battle front that they would have a good luck charm, and they knew that God would never let anything happen to the holy ark.

Sure enough, the day came when the Philistines invaded the land of Israel. The battle ensued. By the middle of the day, the Israelites were running for the hills for the sake of their lives. The Philistines not only won the battle, but they stole the ark of the covenant. So the Philistines brought the ark of the covenant to the city of Ashdod to the house of their god, Dagon. Dagon was their idea of a god. He was an ugly god. He was a merman, that is, half fish and half man.

From that moment, we can only use our imagination. Without doubt, the Philistines were a happy people. There was excitement in the air. They had just defeated the armies of Israel and captured their God. Just imagine the Philistines, in the house of Dagon, bowing down before Dagon, praising and worshipping their idol god. They probably bragged on how great Dagon was and how he had defeated the armies of the Israelites and captured their God. When they were finished, they turned out the light and went home. They came again the next morning and found Dagon laying face down in the earth before the ark of the covenant. How embarrassing to find their god bowing down before the God of Israel. They had to pick Dagon up, dust off his face, and set him on the shelf again. This only shows how depraved and confused man can get when he rejects the true God. Here they are worshipping a god who doesn't have the ability to get up out of the dirt by himself and giving him glory for defeating the armies of Israel.

Once again they fall prostrate before their god Dagon and worship him. The hail him as a great god who defeated the armies of Israel and captured their God. They grow tired, turn out the lights and go home. The next morning, there is Dagon again prostrate before the God of Israel. This time, his head is broken off along with both hands, left unfit for worship by anyone. And this, my friend, is how Dagon committed suicide. Not even super glue can fix the god, Dagon.

Suddenly, the Philistines became plagued with "emerods." The people began to die. They decided that if they did not get it out of their coasts the God of Israel was going to kill them all. So they conjured up the idea of putting the ark on a cart to be pulled by two cows. Along with some gifts, the cows took the cart directly to a camp of the Israelites who were harvesting wheat in a valley. This account is recorded in the book of 1 Samuel, chapters four through six.

Eventually, the ark ended up in the house of a man named Abinadab. It remained there for several years through the reign of King Saul. Once King David was well established in Jerusalem, plans were made to retrieve the ark and bring it to Jerusalem. There was great celebration, along with a large parade with music. However, Israel made a great mistake. They put the ark on a cart to carry it back to Jerusalem. God had made it ever so clear that the ark was absolutely never to be put on a cart. It was holy and could only be carried on the shoulders of the priests. While in route, one of the oxen stumbled, and the ark nearly fell from the cart. One of the keepers named Uzzah reached up to catch the ark. It was sudden and without warning that God struck Uzzah dead on the spot. The wrath of God on Uzzah for illegally touching the ark in movement was totally justified (2 Sam. 6:6-8). Israel was absolutely forbidden from transporting the ark on a cart or wagon. Uzzah's concern and sincerity did not exonerate him from his glaring disobedience of a command of God.

## Traveling with the Ark

Several coverings for the ark were provided to protect it as it was carried from place to place during the journeying of Israel. The specifics of these coverings were given to Moses and recorded in Numbers 4:5-6. It reads:

> And when the camp setteth forward. Aaron shall come, and his sons, and they shall take down the covering vail, and cover the ark of testimony with it:
> And shall put thereon the covering of badgers' skins, and shall spread over it a cloth wholly of blue, and shall put in the staves thereof.

First the ark was wrapped in the "covering vail." This is the vail that separates the Holy Place from the Most Holy Place and is the most precious of all the curtains. Secondly, over the vail was placed the "covering of badgers' skins." And lastly, the external covering of the ark was "a cloth wholly of blue." This was a cloth of fine linen that was dyed blue. This was distinguished from all the other pieces of furniture, for all of them had the badgers' skins for their outer covering. Why then, was the cloth of blue the external garment of the ark? Blue is the color of Heaven and ever employed for the setting forth of heavenly things. This distinguished the ark from all the other pieces of furniture and placed its importance above the others. Further, even in travel, all men would know that the true throne of God is in Heaven. It does not require a spiritual mind to know this fact, but it does take one to see the throne itself.

## What is the Ark?

The Hebrew word translated "ark" actually means "chest, ark, coffin." It is used with reference to a chest or box. In one place it means a money chest (2 Kings 12:9-10), and in another it means a coffin (Gen. 50:26). This is not the same word for Noah's ark and Moses' ark in the bulrushes. These words mean "boat," and this word means "chest."

There are several titles and designations attached to the ark. It was called the "ark of the testimony," so designated because in it were kept the "two tables of testimony" (Ex. 25:22; 31:18). By this name it was most frequently called. It was called the "ark of the covenant" because it contained the covenant Israel agreed to keep with God (Num. 10:33; Judges 20:27; Joshua 3:6). It was named the "ark of the LORD" indicating the great power behind its existence (Joshua 3:13; 4:11). It was titled the "ark of God" associating it with the God of Heaven (1 Sam. 3:3: 5:7). It is designated as the "ark of thy strength" suggesting the authority, power and might of God it represents (Psalm 132:8). Lastly, it is called "the holy ark" which tells of the nature of its use and the character of the God it represents (2 Chron. 35:3).

Around the top perimeter of the box was a crown of gold. The crown served two purposes: to be a symbolical decoration, and to provide a rim that would hold the mercy seat stationary. Crowns are the symbols of sovereignty and power. The ark in the tabernacle was a type of the Lord Jesus Christ in the office of King. The Lord Jesus has three offices consisting of Prophet, Priest and King. In the court of the tabernacle, at the brazen altar, the symbol of the coming Savior, we see and behold the Lord Jesus as the Prophet. A prophet is one who comes from God with God's message for man. The brazen altar and the offerings point to His first coming when He came to die on the cross of Calvary. In the Holy Place, we see Christ as our High Priest. A priest is one who intercedes for the people. In the Holy Place, the priest offered the incense upon the golden altar, and our Lord Jesus Christ is today in the Holy Place in Heaven interceding for us who have believed. But in the Holy of Holies, we meet Christ as the King, as the Sovereign and Almighty. Man crowned Him with thorns, but God has crowned Him with glory and honor (Heb. 2:9).

We are told in the Scriptures that three items were deposited in the ark for safe keeping. We look to a New Testament passage that so informs us: "The ark of the covenant overlaid round about with gold, wherein was the golden pot that had manna, and Aaron's rod that budded, and the tables of the covenant" (Heb. 9:4).

According to 1 Kings 8:9 and 2 Chronicles 5:10 when the ark was placed in the Temple, the only item in the ark was the two tables of stone. Hebrews 9:4 speaks of the contents of the ark during the days that it was lodged in the tabernacle and was in the wilderness journey; whereas, these other passages tell us what comprised its contents after it came to rest in the Temple. It is abundantly clear that the manna and rod were removed at some time before it was placed in the Temple.

## Three Items In The Ark

### Manna

The first item mentioned in the ark was the golden pot that had the manna. Manna was the bread God sent down from Heaven to feed the children of Israel on their way to the Promised Land (Ex. 16:11-31). Each morning the Israelites went out and gathered one omer for every person in his family of this white substance they called manna. On the sixth day, they gathered and prepared enough to last through the Sabbath day. They were supplied this bread throughout the wilderness wandering. The record of the manna being placed in the ark is found in Exodus 16:32-34 which reads:

> And Moses said, This is the thing which the LORD commandeth, Fill an omer of it to be kept for your generations; that they may see the bread wherewith I have fed you in the wilderness, when I brought you forth from the land of Egypt.
> And Moses said unto Aaron, Take a pot, and put an omer full of manna therein, and lay it up before the LORD, to be kept for your generations.
> As the LORD commanded Moses, so Aaron laid it up  before the Testimony, to be kept.

Since the manna had sustained the lives of the Israelites in the wilderness, it was a fitting symbol of Jesus Christ who sustains our lives spiritually. It was a sign of Christ's faithfulness in caring for His own. When Jesus emphasized that He was the Bread of Life in John chapter six, He contrasted Himself with the manna that came down in the wilderness. It reads:

> I am that bread of life.
> Your fathers did eat manna in the wilderness, and are dead.

This is the bread which cometh down from heaven,
that a man may eat thereof, and not die.

I am the living bread which came down from heav-
en: if any man eat of this bread. he shall live for ever:
and the bread that I will give is my flesh, which I will
give for the life of the world.

John 6:48-51

Those who ate the manna in the wilderness eventually all died, but those who partake of Jesus Christ live forever. Thus, the manna in the ark of the covenant presented Christ as the great provider and sustainer of life. The
golden pot seems to emphasize the divine glory of Him
who became the food of His people.

## Aaron's Rod That Budded

The second item in the ark was "Aaron's rod that budded." There was a revolt in Israel against Moses and Aaron
led by a man named Korah. The record of that revolt is found
in Numbers 16 and 17. That the Lord might establish the
priesthood of Aaron against all controversy, He required that
a rod should be taken from each tribe with the name of the
head of the tribe written on it. Aaron's name was written on
his rod who represented the tribe of Levi. The rods were
placed in the tabernacle before the ark. Here then were
twelve dead sticks allowed to be overnight. "And it came to
pass, that on the morrow Moses went into the tabernacle of
witness; and, behold, the rod of Aaron for the house of Levi
was budded, and brought forth buds, and bloomed blossoms,
and yielded almonds" (Num. 17:8).

This living rod was not only an avouchment of the priesthood of Aaron, but a symbolic prophecy of the priesthood of
our Lord. The Lord vindicated Aaron by causing the dead rod
to live. The Lord fully vindicated His Son by raising Him
from the dead. Being raised from the dead, "he ever liveth to
make intercession" for us (Heb. 7:25). This rod declares

that the high priest that represents man must be able to give life to that which is dead. As life was given to that dead rod, so Christ is able to give life to a dead soul. This rod that budded, blossomed and bore fruit was a witness that the Son of God had the power to rise again from death and is the continual source of life to all who should believe and trust in Him.

Moses was instructed to take Aaron's rod and place it in the ark. "And the LORD said unto Moses, Bring Aaron's rod again before the testimony, to be kept for a token against the rebels; and thou shalt quite take away their murmurings from me, that they die not" (Num. 17:10).

## The Two Tables of Stone

The third item found in the ark was the two tables of stone containing the Ten Commandments. Actually this was the most significant of the items and the first to be deposited in the ark. The other two items were added later, but the tables of stone were placed in the ark from the beginning. When the other items were later removed, the tables of stone remained.

It was called the "ark of the covenant" because it contained these tables of Law which was the covenant into which the people entered at Sinai. Moses broke the first tables of Law when he came down from the mount and found the people in idolatry (Ex. 32:19). However, God later told Moses, "I will write on the tables the words that were in the first tables which thou brakest, and thou shalt put them in the ark" (Deut. 10:2).

The second set of tables of Law set forth God's unbroken covenant in the midst of an erring people. God's righteous standards are represented in them and because those standards could never be lowered. The tables of stone were placed in the ark as a constant reminder to the Israelites. The tables of Law represented God's perfect standard of government and judgment and the penalty for violating them.

These tables of Law actually condemned the people. They had already proven in the breaking of the first tables that they could not live up to God's perfect standard and keep the laws. These laws sets forth the requirements man must meet in order to live and associate with God. They also set forth the penalty for violating any one of them. "Cursed is every one that continueth not in all things which are written in the book of the law to do them" (Gal. 3:10). "For whosoever shall keep the whole law, and yet offend in one point, he is guilty of all" (James 2:10).

The Law could not save; it could only condemn. It could not take away sin; it could only reveal sin. It could not give life to the sinner; it could only kill the transgressor. The ark, therefore, by itself was a throne of judgment, condemning the sinner, demanding his death and eternal banishment from the presence of God. "The LORD reigneth; let the people tremble: he sitteth between the cherubims" (Psalm 99:1).

The picture presented in the ark is that of gloom and despair to sinful man. It only speaks of our hopelessness. The entire world has broken the laws and comes under the condemnation of it. All are judged guilty and must be punished by death. "There is none righteous, no, not one" (Rom. 3:10). "All have sinned, and come short of the glory of God" (Rom. 3:23).

Since the ark was made of wood overlaid with gold, inside and outside, it speaks of the twofold nature of Christ, His humanity and His deity. By virtue of this fact, it also indicates that Christ Himself will be the eternal Judge.

It has been suggested that each of the articles contained in the ark was a reminder and a witness of failure on the part of the people. The tables of Law reminded them of the golden calf and their failure to keep the Law. The manna reminded them of their murmuring and unbelief. And the rod that budded recalled their rebellion against God and each other.

# CHAPTER THIRTEEN

# MERCY AT
# THE MERCY SEAT

And thou shalt make a mercy seat [of] pure gold: two cubits and a half [shall be] the length thereof, and a cubit and a half the breadth thereof.

And thou shalt make two cherubims [of] gold, [of] beaten work shalt thou make them, in the two ends of the mercy seat.

And make one cherub on the one end, and the other cherub on the other end: [even] of the mercy seat shall ye make the cherubims on the two ends thereof.

And the cherubims shall stretch forth [their] wings on high, covering the mercy seat with their wings, and their faces [shall look] one to another; toward the mercy seat shall the faces of the cherubims be.

And thou shalt put the mercy seat above upon the ark; and in the ark thou shalt put the testimony that I shall give thee.

**Exodus 25:17-21; Exodus 37:6-9**

# THE MERCY SEAT

The mercy seat is considered by many a distinct piece of furniture from the ark, but their association is so close that they actually appear as one piece. The details for the construction of the mercy seat are given in Exodus 25:17-21.

The mercy seat was a slab of pure gold, forty-five inches (two and one-half cubits) long by twenty-seven inches (one and one-half cubits) wide. The thickness is not given. A cherub was beaten of gold and placed on each end of the seat. They bowed inward toward each other with their faces to the mercy seat. Their wings were lifted up above their heads forming a canopy of wings. No wood was used in their construction.

The mercy seat was the lid of the ark of the covenant. It was exactly the same length and width of the ark. When placed on the ark, it sat in a groove formed by the crown of gold around the top edge.

## Meaning of the Mercy Seat

The word translated "mercy seat" is the Hebrew *kapporeth*. This word is derived from the root word *kaphar*. The word *kapporeth* means "covering for the ark, the mercy seat." The root word *kaphar* means "to cover over sin, to pardon, to forgive, to appease, pacify, to be expiated, to hide, to make atonement and propitiation." Hence, the word translated "mercy seat" is derived from the same root as the word "atonement" found with the sacrificial offerings and in the phrase "day of atonement."

Actually, the root word from which we get mercy seat is most commonly translated "atonement." It is used in connection with the burnt-offering (Lev. 1:4; 14:20; 16:24), the trespass-offering (Lev. 5:16, 18); the sin-offering (Lev. 4:20, 26, 31, 35) and numerous other respects. There is a definite connection between the usage of the words translated "atonement" and "mercy seat."

The Greek word equivalent in the New Testament to the Hebrew word for mercy seat is *hilaskomai*. The Septuagint translates the Hebrew *kapporeth* to the Greek *hilaskomai*. The Greek *hilaskomai* means "propitiate, merciful." These words, though one Hebrew and the other Greek, appear to be identical and completely interchangeable in meaning.

In the New Testament, the word from which we get "mercy seat" is translated several ways. In Hebrews 9:5 it is appropriately rendered "mercyseat." In 1 John 2:2 and 1 John 4:10 it is translated "propitiation." And the same word appears as "merciful" in Luke 18:13.

The generally accepted significance of the word for mercy seat is "to cover," or "to cover up." It must be understood that the word does not mean to cover up in the sense of trying to hide. That which is hid is never God or anything godly. According to the general opinion, the covering removed the sins from the sight of the Lord; that the Lord saw them no more; that they no longer provoked His anger and punishment. This is not the true meaning intended in this case.

The atonement does not have the meaning of trying to hide or conceal sin or to cause a sin not to have been committed. The real meaning is that it deprives sin of its power to come between us and God. It is so complete, effectual and overpowering a covering that all real and active force in that which is covered up is thereby rendered impossible or slain. It is a process in the sight of God in which the sin is rendered harmless. It is equivalent to canceling and utterly annihilation. While the ark reveals the attribute of God in justice and righteousness, the mercy seat reveals the attribute of grace and mercy.

## Cherubim On The Mercy Seat

The cherubim were on the mercy seat and formed an essential part of it. The cherubim represent supremacy and power. In the logic of symbols, the cherubim on the mercy seat testify that Jesus Christ on the throne of God has power and supremacy over all.

Cherubim are the highest among the angelic order of creatures. The first time they are mentioned, they are viewed guarding the way to the tree of life. They are seen in two separate visions of Heaven as surrounding the throne of God ready to execute God's will. Essentially they are messengers of judgment. Here on the mercy seat, they stand poised to strike were it not for the blood-sprinkled mercy seat.

The mercy seat was thus the cover of the ark, and both together formed one vessel of the sanctuary. Each has distinguishing spiritual meanings, but the greater significance lies in the two units as one. The ark represents justice and righteousness and the lid represents mercy and grace. It is here that judgment and mercy can meet. It is here in the Most Holy Place that "mercy and truth are met together; righteousness and peace have kissed each other" (Psalm 85:10). It is before the ark and mercy seat that the penalty of judgment is paid and that God is appeased and offers mercy and grace to mankind.

### The Highest Altar

In every sense of the meaning, the mercy seat was an altar. In fact, the highest and most perfect expiation was effected upon it. Just as the blood of the ordinary sacrifices were sprinkled upon the altar of burnt-offering and the altar of incense, the mercy seat was shown to be an altar. But it was an altar that was much higher and holier than the other two altars just as the Most Holy Place was higher and holier than the Holy Place and the court of the tabernacle. The throne of God being an altar must have been truly the throne of grace.

The ark without the mercy seat is no more than a throne of judgment. A nation of transgressors could never stand before the naked Law. When the Philistines sent back the ark which God had suffered to fall into their hands, we are told:

> And he smote the men of Beth-shemesh, because they had looked into the ark of the LORD, even he smote of the people fifty thousand and threescore and ten men: and the people lamented, because the Lord had smitten many of the people with a great slaughter.
>
> And the men of Beth-shemesh said, Who is able to stand before this holy LORD God? and to whom shall he go up from us?"
>
> 1 Samuel 6: 19-20

In order to "look into the ark," the mercy seat had to be removed, and in removing it, they exposed the Law and thus severed mercy from judgment; the result of which must ever be death for the guilty.

## Activities on the Day of Atonement

There was a definite connection between the Day of Atonement, the ark and the mercy seat. On this day, the high priest put aside his special garments, bathed completely at the laver, and put on simple white linen garments (Lev. 16:4). He first offered sacrifices to make atonement for himself and the priests (Lev. 16:6). He then slew one of two goats, the other being a scapegoat. This goat served as a sin-offering for the entire nation of Israel. The high priest would enter into the Holy Place and sprinkle blood before the vail, then he would push aside the vail and enter the Most Holy Place. He would step before the ark and mercy seat and sprinkle the blood of the sin offering one time on the mercy seat and seven times before them (Lev. 16:14-15). Upon God's acceptance of the offering, He would appear between the cherubim in the cloud or as it is commonly called, the shekinah light (Lev. 16:2).

The high priest had a great responsibility in his performance of duties on this Day of Atonement. He went into the Most Holy Place representing a sinful and unrighteous people; a people who had broken all the laws and precepts of the Lord. According to the law in the ark, they must be punished by death. The high priest did not approach the ark and mercy seat and argue in behalf of the people that they were basically good and had not intentionally done evil. Instead, he approached the ark and mercy seat confessing the ungodliness and wretchedness of the people. He confessed that they deserved the wrath and judgment of God.

How could this high priest appease an angry God and make reconciliation for a people so sinful? How could he make such wicked beings acceptable to a righteous God? How could the high priest make unfavorable man favorable to the eyes of the Lord? As the priest approached the ark and mercy seat, he dipped his fingers in the basin of blood from the sin-offering and sprinkled the blood once on the mercy seat and then sprinkled it seven times in front of them. When God would look down upon the ark and the mercy seat, He did not see the laws and the penalties; He saw the blood. As God looked down and saw the blood on the door of the homes of the Israelites in Egypt and was merciful, He looked down at the blood on the mercy seat and was merciful. The blood was the proof, the evidence, the receipt that the judgment and penalty of sin had been paid. The debt of sin was settled and it appeased the Lord. He could extend mercy and grace to mankind.

This is not without spiritual significance. Hebrews 9:7-26 makes it ever so clear that the work of the priest on the

Day of Atonement was symbolical of the atoning death of Christ. Jesus Christ is both the Priest and the Sacrifice. After His death and resurrection, Jesus appeared before the very throne of God in Heaven and before the Lord Himself and offered His own blood as atonement for the sins of mankind. It is as though He stepped before the Father with a basin filled with His own blood and said: "Father, here is my blood. Here is the payment for the sins of mankind. Here is the proof that the penalty of death has been made!" No greater proof can be made that the penalty of death has been executed than the presentation of the blood of the victim. "Neither by the blood of goats and calves, but by his own blood he entered in once into the holy place, having obtained eternal redemption for us" (Heb. 9:12).

"Herein is love, not that we loved God, but that he loved us, and sent his Son to be the propitiation (mercy seat) for our sins" (1 John 4:10). When the sinner of Luke 18 prayed "God be merciful to me a sinner" (verse 13), he was literally praying "On the basis of the offering made at the mercy seat, be merciful to me a sinner."

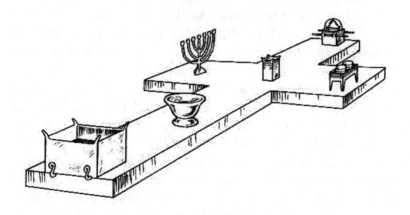

**The layout of the furniture has the same shape as a cross.**

Among the instructions given for the mercy seat, God told Moses: "There I will meet with thee, and I will commune with thee from above the mercy seat, from between the two cherubims which are upon the ark of the testimony, of all things which I will give thee in commandment unto the children of Israel" (Ex. 25:22). Alluding to the Lord at the mercy seat, the psalmist said: "thou that dwellest between the cherubims, shine forth" (Psalm 80:1).

Christian literature often speaks of the shekinah that appeared between the cherubim above the mercy seat. The term shekinah never appears in the Scriptures, but it is used in much literature as a synonymous word for scriptural terms such as "glory." When the shekinah light is said to appear between the cherubim, it is meant that the presence and glory of God is there.

The question is raised: Is there an actual light that appears between the cherubim? Psalm 80:1 says that the Lord will "shine forth" from between the cherubim. It seems that when God spoke from above the mercy seat that there was a cloud or light that would shine forth. If we understand terms we might appropriately address it as the shekinah light or shekinah glory.

As the high priest sprinkled the blood upon the mercy seat, no doubt, the Lord appeared many times in this cloud or light to express His approval of the offering and to impart His word to Israel through the mediator.

# APPENDIX

And they came, every one whose heart stirred him up, and every one whom his spirit made willing, [and] they brought the LORD'S offering to the work of the tabernacle of the congregation, and for all his service, and for the holy garments.

And they came, both men and women, as many as were willing hearted, [and] brought bracelets, and earrings, and rings, and tablets, all jewels of gold: and every man that offered [offered] an offering of gold unto the LORD.

And every man, with whom was found blue, and purple, and scarlet, and fine linen, and goats' [hair], and red skins of rams, and badgers' skins, brought [them].

Every one that did offer an offering of silver and brass brought the LORD'S offering: and every man, with whom was found shittim wood for any work of the service, brought [it].

And all the women that were wise hearted did spin with their hands, and brought that which they had spun, [both] of blue, and of purple, [and] of scarlet, and of fine linen.

And all the women whose heart stirred them up in wisdom spun goats' [hair].

And the rulers brought onyx stones, and stones to be set, for the ephod, and for the breastplate;

And spice, and oil for the light, and for the anointing oil, and for the sweet incense.

The children of Israel brought a willing offering unto the LORD, every man and woman, whose heart made them willing to bring for all manner of work, which the LORD had commanded to be made by the hand of Moses.

**Exodus 35:21-29**

# MISCELLANEOUS TOPICS

## The Dedication of the Tabernacle

The tabernacle was reared up the first day of the first month of the second year in the history of that nation (Ex. 12:2; 40:2). It was exactly one year to the day from the time God instructed Israel to prepare for the Passover in Egypt until the tabernacle was dedicated. The actual construction took approximately seven months.

The fortieth chapter of Exodus is devoted to the set up of the tabernacle. The words are repeatedly stated: "As the Lord commanded Moses." The structure was erected and the furniture was placed inside. The building, the furniture, the accessories and the priests were all anointed with the holy anointing oil. As Moses was carrying out these commands, the Lord spoke to Moses from the mercy seat (Num. 7:89).

The altar was furnished with wood and the appointed sacrifices; the laver was filled with pure water. The candlestick lamps were lit; bread and wine were put on the table of shewbread; and incense was offered on the golden altar.

Aaron and his sons were consecrated according to the laws of the priests. They came to the laver and washed themselves and dressed themselves before ministering to the things of the tabernacle.

All the while, princes representing each of the twelve tribes of the nation were bringing special gifts consisting of wagons and oxen for the transporting of the tabernacle. For twelve days more they continued to bring other special gifts consisting of accessories, incense, oil, animals, flour and such (Num. 7:1-88).

"Then a cloud covered the tent of the congregation, and the glory of the Lord filled the tabernacle" (Ex. 40:34). It was at even time, or approximately six o'clock in the evening, that the cloud filled the tabernacle and remained until the morning (Num. 9:15). The house was built, dedicated and filled with the glory of God. God had come to dwell among them. What a glorious event it must have been for Moses and the people of Israel!

## The History of the Tabernacle

The first day of the month of Nisan (or Abib) was established by the Lord as the first day of the religious year for the Israelites (Ex. 12:2). On the fifteenth day of this month the Israelites began their journey from Egypt (Ex. 16:1). In the third month of their exodus, they arrived at the base of Mt. Sinai (Ex. 19:1). Nearly two months went by as Moses spent much time on the mountain receiving the blueprints for the system of worship for the Israelites (Ex. 24:18). Approximately seven more months were spent in the actual construction of the tabernacle. Exactly one year from the date God instituted the religious new year, and eleven and one-half months from the exodus, the tabernacle was erected and dedicated (Ex. 40:2, 17).

After sitting at the base of Mt. Sinai for some fifty days, the tabernacle encountered its first move (Num. 10:11). It gradually moved through the wilderness of Paran on to Kadesh-barnea. Because of the report of the spies and the murmuring of the people, the Israelites remained in the wilderness for a total of forty years. Of this time, over thirty-five years were spent at Kadesh. Because history deals mainly with the unusual, the daily occurrences at the tabernacle were hardly mentioned.

After the crossing of the Jordan River and during the conquest of Canaan, the tabernacle at first was temporarily located at Gilgal (Joshua 4:19; 5:10; 9:6; 10:6, 43). This seems to have been the headquarters for Joshua's conquest of the land of Canaan. This site was temporary, and in time, the tabernacle was moved to Shiloh in Ephraim

(Joshua 18:1; 19:51). This was a central location conven-
ient for the men to attend the three annual pilgrimage
feasts. The sanctuary remained there throughout the period of the judges, a span of about three hundred years.
During the period of the judges, Israel repeatedly fell into
apostasy, and the tabernacle services must have been performed in a formal, heartless manner, if at all. By the time
of the last judge, Samuel, the tabernacle appears to have
had some permanent features such as doors and posts (1
Sam. 1:9; 3:15). Furthermore, the tabernacle had come to
be called a "temple" (1 Sam. 1:9; 3:3). It is entirely possible that over a period of years with regular maintenance
and sitting in one location that certain adjustments were
made to it.

When war erupted with the Philistines in Samuel's
time, the Israelites were facing defeat during the battle of
Ebenezer (1 Sam. 4:1-2). The people decided to bring the
ark of the covenant from Shiloh to the battle front that it
might be some lucky charm to them to win the battle
(verses 3-9). The outcome was tragic. Israel not only lost
the war to the Philistines, but they also lost the ark of the
covenant (verses 10-11). The story of the ark of the
covenant in the hands of the Philistines is filled with sad-
ness and humor. In all, the ark was in the hands of the
Philistines for seven months (1 Sam. 6:1).

The subsequent history of the tabernacle is somewhat
obscure. The next reference of it is at Nob with Ahimelech
as high priest (1 Sam. 21:2; 22:11). Sometime after Saul
had slain the priests, the tabernacle was removed to
Gibeon (1 Chron. 16:39; 21:29).

After David was fully established as the king of Israel,
he wished to institute the tabernacle worship in his capi-
tal city of Jerusalem. He prepared a place for the ark and
pitched a tabernacle in the tradition of the original at
Gibeon (2 Sam. 6:17; 1 Chron. 16:1). David along with a
great host of people, went to Kirjath-jearim to get the ark.
It was a great party with many musicians playing along

the way (2 Sam. 6:1-5). The ark was placed upon a newly
made cart, which was a mistake, because the ark was to
be carried only by the staves borne by the priests. Along
the way, the oxen shook the ark and Uzzah reached out
and took hold of the ark to stabilize it. When he did, God
struck him dead (verses 6-7). The thing put fear in the
heart of David, and he left it in the home of Obed-edom
the Gittite (verses 9-11). After three months, the ark was
brought to Jerusalem and placed in the tabernacle David
built.

With David's removal of the ark to Jerusalem, there
were two tabernacles: a tabernacle with its altar at
Gibeon and another with the ark in Jerusalem. The sacrifices were still being offered on the altar at the tabernacle
in Gibeon at the time David determined to build the
Temple (1 Chron. 16:39; 21:29). This was several years
after David built the tabernacle and placed the ark in it in
the city of Jerusalem (1 Chron. 15:1-29). After Solomon's
Temple was built, the tabernacle, the ark and all its
equipment were brought into the Temple (1 Kings 8:4).
Only the ark of the covenant and mercy seat were used in
the new Temple. It appears that the tabernacle, the furniture and the accessories were kept as sacred relics in the
Temple. Thus, the tabernacle disappeared from history.

## What Has Happened to the Ark?

Does the original ark of the covenant and the mercy
seat exist in modern time? There is a great deal of speculation concerning its existence. The final conclusion is
that if it does exist, few, if any, people know where it is.

In the mid 1930's, several articles appeared claiming
that the ark was possibly in Ethiopia. The story is that
when the Queen of Sheba went to visit King Solomon, she
returned home and had a son by him. His name was
Menelik. There is a very strong claim by many of the
black race that they are the descendants of Solomon and

to this day claim the Jewish religion. The story goes on to say that when Menelik became a young man, he went to Palestine to visit his father, Solomon. It is said that Solomon was so pleased with the boy that he had made for him an exact reproduction of the ark. But the boy, having inherited some of his father's wisdom, gave the priests of the temple a farewell party, got them all drunk and then substituted the replica for the original, which he carried back to Ethiopia. It is supposed to rest in some church in Askum. There have been some television documentaries regarding this position. The modern religious Jew does not take this position serious.

Jews have considered another position. Some believe that when the roman General, Titus, invaded and destroyed Jerusalem in A.D. 70, he may have taken the ark back to Rome with him. The Catholic Church and the Pope emphatically deny that they have the ark of the covenant.

Through the years, in various places, people have come forward and claimed that they have seen the ark of the covenant, but to no proof.

There is an ancient Hebrew tradition as to the whereabouts of the ark. This position is that at the time of the Babylonian capture of Jerusalem, Jeremiah the prophet took it and hid it in a cave. This claim is made in 2 Maccabees 2:4-8 which states:

> It was also contained in the same writing, that the prophet, being warned of God, commanded the tabernacle and the ark to go with him, as he went forth into the mountain, where Moses climbed up, and saw the heritage of God.
>
> And when Jeremy came thither, he found an hollow cave, wherein he laid the tabernacle, and the ark, and the altar of incense, and so stopped the door.
>
> And some of those that followed him came to mark the way, but they could not find it.

Which when Jeremy perceived, he blamed them, saying, As far that place, it shall be unknown until the time that God gather his people again together, and receive them unto mercy.

Then shall the Lord shew them these things, and the glory of the Lord shall appear, and the cloud also, as it was shewed under Moses, and as when Solomon desired that the place might be honourably sanctified.

In recent history, a tunnel has been excavated along the western wall of the temple mount. It has been excavated to street level at the time of Christ. Along the wall there is evidence of arch ways that enter through the wall and under the temple mount. These arches have been blocked up prior to the invasion by Rome. A Rabbi sneaked into the tunnel, removed a block and went under the temple mount. While under there, he claimed to have seen the ark of the covenant before being forced out. Due to the political problems in the Middle East this claim cannot be confirmed.

There is no Biblical proof that the ark of the covenant will reappear in the last days. After all, true temple worship will not be restored until Christ appears for the millennial reign. He will return and built His own temple in Jerusalem and will rule and reign with His saints. Jesus will be in the Holy of Holies. There will not necessarily be the need for the ark. We will just have to wait and see if the ark should ever be discovered. Consequently, we do not know where the ark of the covenant is located.

# Bibliography

Halderman, I. M. The Tabernacle, *Priesthood and Offerings*. Fleming H. Revell Company, Old Tapan, New Jersey.

Strong, James. *The Tabernacle of Israel*. Kregel Publications, Grand Rapids, Michigan.

_____. *Apocrypha, II Maccabees*. Cambridge University Press, New York, New York.

_____. *Smith's Bible Dictionary*, Zondervan Publishing House, Grand Rapids, Michigan.